The Dearest Freshness Deep Down Things

THE DEAREST FRESHNESS
DEEP DOWN THINGS

An Introduction to the
Philosophy of Being

PIERRE-MARIE EMONET, O.P.

Translated by
Robert R. Barr

A Herder & Herder Book
The Crossroad Publishing Company
New York

The Crossroad Publishing Company
370 Lexington Avenue, New York, NY 10017

Original edition: *Une métaphysique pour les simples.*
© 1993 by Éditions C.L.D., Chambray-lès-Tours, France

English translation © 1999 by The Crossroad Publishing Company

Printed in the United States of America

Library of Congress Cataloging-in-Publication Data

Emonet, Pierre-Marie.
    [Métaphysique pour les simples.   English]
    The dearest freshness deep down things : an introduction to the philosophy of being / Pierre-Marie Emonet : translated by Robert R. Barr.
       p.   cm.
    ISBN 0-8245-1794-6 (pbk.)
    1. Metaphysics.   2. Neo-Scholasticism.   I. Title.
BD131.E4813   1999
110—dc21   99-31417
                                          CIP

1   2   3   4   5   6   7   8   9   10   03   02   01   00   99

God's Grandeur

The world is charged with the grandeur of God.
It will flame out, like shining from shook foil;
It gathers to a greatness, like the ooze of oil
Crushed. Why do men then now not reck his rod?
Generations have trod, have trod, have trod;
And all is seared with trade; bleared, smeared with toil;
And wears man's smudge and shares man's smell: the soil
Is bare now, nor can foot feel, being shod.

And for all this, nature is never spent;
There lives the dearest freshness deep down things;
And though the last lights off the black West went
Oh, morning, at the brown brink eastward, springs–
Because the Holy Ghost over the bent
World broods with warm breast and with ah! bright wings.

–Gerard Manley Hopkins

Contents

Part 2

Part 1

A sensitivity of the intelligence to being is an incomparably precious gift.
—Dom Vermeil

For me, the true poet is the metaphysician.
—Père H. Clérissac, O.P.

Introduction

The contemplative is not one who discovers secrets no one knows, but one who is swept into ecstasy by what everyone knows.

—A Carthusian

W E PLACE THIS QUOTATION at the beginning of our book because it best describes the goal we pursue in these pages. We should like to show the reader how it was in sounding the depths of the primary data of the intelligence common to us all that the philosophers of ancient Greece were able to tap the source of philosophical wisdom. They demonstrated that the evidences of intellectual awareness are pregnant with the most profound truths—the truths that possess the capacity to lead the spirit to God.

Our intent, then, is to set the reader on the path to these depths. We mean to do so using a minimum of the scholarly vocabulary in which this knowledge is ordinarily couched. We are writing for "beginners," who have not been initiated into the methods of scholasticism. They must not think that this shortcoming is fatal, or that it will keep them forever at a distance from the limpid spring of philosophical truth.

We remembered that the first awakening of philosophical

thought, in the seventh and sixth centuries B.C., occurred in poetry. Philosophical intuition and poetic intuition were exquisitely intertwined. Could we retrace that path to arrive at the first truths? And we made the attempt.

What a wonderful surprise it was to discover that, indeed, the metaphysician and the poet are siblings in the intuitions that open up to the mind and spirit the domain of an erstwhile primordial darkness! Perhaps, then, the best way to introduce the reader to philosophy will be to ask poetry—as was done in the birth of philosophy—to raise philosophical understanding aloft on its wings and bear it more rapidly to the truths of its realm: especially and first of all to that which is *being* in things—the absolutely first "act" that things perform. Indeed, it is from this *act of being* that the threads emerge that bind things to God.

It was not quotations that we sought among the poets, but their intuitions, which are so close to, sometimes even identical with, those of the philosophers. To meet the poets on these heights cannot fail to transport philosophers with joy. To give ear to their song stirs them to simplify their language, to retreat from too weighty a technical style. Then the philosopher is engaged in the same adventure as the poet:

> To give a purer sense to the words of the tribe.
> —Mallarmé, *Le Tombeau d'Edgar Poe*

1

The Original Meaning of Being

To give a purer sense to the words of the tribe.
—Mallarmé

A METAPHYSICAL UNDERSTANDING is awakened in a person the day she or he wonders what it is to "be." It is "being," in the things of nature, contemplated for itself, that reveals the truly authentic metaphysician. This may be an astonishing statement. How could this most banal, most worn-out word of all be the luminous center of a knowledge as profound and universal as metaphysics?

For the philosopher, precisely the verb "be" is neither banal nor worn-out. But in order to find its true denotation, we must seek its source. Here is how we can discover that source. Let us conjugate the verb "be" in the present indicative, third person singular: "he/she/it *is*." Now, the word "is" has come down to us from the lost ancient Indo-European language that is also the ancestor of ancient Sanskrit. But in Sanskrit "is" is *asti*. And *asti* means "is of itself, maintains itself independently."

As we see, the verb "be," which designates the object of the metaphysician's contemplation, is by no means banal, as if it denoted the simple fact of a thing's being in a given place at a given time. Those who invented this word wished, instead, to signify the first act by which a thing, and all things, "hold themselves erect," "hold fast," "stand firm." "Be," then, denotes the activity that things perform in order to "hold fast in themselves," over against other things that perform the same act for themselves.

The act of holding fast in oneself and from a point of departure in oneself, which is the act performed, for example, by the living being, is the foundation of everything else. All other activities suppose this one, without which everything would collapse. Now, it is before this primordial effort in things that the metaphysician experiences an inexhaustible wonder. Would it be possible to express in words the kind of awe that is born in the spirit when it perceives, at the core of things, this absolutely first act?

A passage in Paul Claudel's play *The Golden Head* would seem to respond to this desire. Here is how the poet addresses the old tree that, since his adolescence, has lavished upon him such an important lesson:

> But as for you, you are but a continual striving, with the diligent straining of your body beyond inanimate matter. How you, ancient one, suck the earth, thrusting and opening on all sides your strong, sensuous roots! And the sky—how you stretch toward it! And how you bend utterly to its breath, in boundless foliage, O form of fire! What inexhaustible soil in the clutch of all of the roots of your being, and the infinite sky, together with the sun and the stars in their annual round, when you take hold with your mouth, made of all your arms, with the cluster of your branches, grasping everything in you that breathes! Earth and sky, you need them both completely, in order to maintain yourself erect. Would that I might stand so erect![1]

It would be difficult to find a better expression of that primal effort exerted by things in order—as the poet says, going back to the original sense of being—*to maintain themselves erect.* To be sure, in the old tree this effort is spectacular. Still, in all things, and in proportion to their nature, the metaphysician admires a similar basic activity.

2

The Radiant Thrust of Being

*All things eagerly hasten toward being more,
in the light of the morning.*

—Francis Olivier

THE GREEK THINKERS who came before Socrates gave birth to metaphysics when they posed the question: What is the *being* of things? And they answered: the first of the acts that they perform. But we must add at once that what most captivated them in this "being" was the birth of things—the phase of their arising. Let us say: *being in its past.*

The pre-Socratics gave the *being* of the things of nature, in the inaugural phase of this being, the name *physis*—Greek for "nature." This is the category of all of the fragments that have come down to us from these philosophers' works.

Here again, if we wish really to connect with the intuition of these early thinkers, we must rediscover the original meaning of the verb "be," but this time in the past tense. In romance languages, "was" is rendered by *fu-*. *Fu-* comes from the Latin *fuit,* "was," which comes in turn from the Greek *phyein.* And this form is a cousin of the Sanskrit *bhu.* Now, in Sanskrit, this verb denotes the act by which a thing thrusts forth to the light,

8

for example, the act of a seed when it is differentiated into organs, or of an egg when it develops into an embryo. Another example would be the act of a seed becoming petals. Do we not call an embryo a "fetus" (from the Greek *phyton,* or *futon*) once it has acquired the characteristics typical of its species?

Even more than by the act of "standing fast," standing on its own, it is by the act of thrusting outside matter that a thing deserves the name of "being." It is now from a point of departure in itself that it will "stand fast in itself." Now, there is a phase of "being" in which being emerges from itself, in which it extracts from itself the power to give itself the organs that will assure its survival. The first Greek philosophers were fascinated by this power of "emergence," this radiant, or radiating, thrust of the flower, the bird, the little human being, as they come forth into the light.

It is not necessary, fortunately, to have one's name in a philosophical dictionary in order to enjoy this metaphysical intuition! It is marvelously expressed by a poet like Charles-Ferdinand Ramuz, whose gaze was frequently beckoned by these depths:

> I write these lines at the approach of Eastertide, as the world of beings grouped around me is in its resurrection. Its revival is by fits and starts, from a state in which it was, to another state, in which it was not quite; and from death to life. All things eagerly hasten toward being more, in the light of the morning. They are encouraged by the light over their heads, calling to them, "Come here, where I am." Everywhere is singing. The singing had stopped. And the mysterious shoot springs up between two clumps in the garden, pink, weak and strong, weaker than all else beside, stronger than all else beside.[2]

And there you have it! A modern Swiss poet, writing like a pre-Socratic!

3

The Labor of Being

*Look, listen, and then breathe, for all being is
impelled. . . . It is the sap, the great circulation
that is in the trunks, in the least stems.*
   —Charles-Ferdinand Ramuz, "Easter Song"

CLAUDEL AND RAMUZ both experience a genuine awe
with regard to things. They convey their sense of the mystery of things in that poorest of words, "is": but for them, the verb "to be" means the labor performed by things in order to push themselves beyond matter, and having accomplished that, to keep themselves there. "But as for you," says Claudel to the tree, "you are but a continual striving." And Ramuz celebrates the little shoot, "weak and strong, weaker than all else beside, stronger than all else beside." In the great body of a tree, or in a miniscule seed, what strikes our two poets first and foremost is the energy unfolding in them. "Energy." Would that be another name for being?

Aristotle (fourth century B.C.) was the first to make this identification. He delved more deeply into the intuitions of the first Greek philosophers, who had already sought to express what constitutes the *being* of things.

As he analyzed the process of the genesis of plants and animals, Aristotle was struck especially by their work, their labor. He called it, in Greek, *energeia* (from *en,* "in, within," and *erg,* "work"). As it pushes out of its seed, the flower accomplishes a labor within itself. Then this force of labor within the plant organizes the materials according to the various organs of the plant. The *force* in question here is not that which causes the plant to act on its surroundings, or causes the bird to fly. It is that force, altogether antecedent and interior, that gives the plant "to be" (*Metaphysics* 9.8; 1050a22). It is that force that has caused it to construct itself, then to appear, to win its presence in the world.

And so it appeared to Aristotle that what constitutes the being of things is actually a prime energy, a first energy. The words "be" and "being" cannot express adequately, just by themselves, what they imply. We must invent other words, besides, in order to express all of the meanings with which this unique term, "being," is charged.

This power of labor implied in being will best be characterized if we call it a legislative power, not an executive one. It is the power possessed by the "creative idea." The idea that presides over the organized development of a living seed resembles the creative idea of a work of art. The idea, the spiritual seed, does not perform physical actions, but it arouses actions, and directs them, leads them to their goal (*Meta.* 9.3; 1047a30).

The first philosophers expressed this thrust of the living seed toward the light by the term that was to become a technical one: *physis.* What this word meant is marvelously illustrated by an illustrious poet in the work of a tree that grows by chance in an abandoned house. The house was a windowless shelter. The tree had gone in search of light:

> This tree, born blind, had spread out its powerful musculature in the night and groped from one wall to another, and staggered, and the drama had been imprinted in its twisted trunk.

Then, having broken an attic window in the direction of the sun, it had burst forth, straight as a column. I witnessed the movements of its victory with the detached perspective of the historian. Contrasting magnificently with the knots gathered by the effort of its trunk in its coffin, it now spread itself out in the calm, displaying its foliage grandly, like a table where the sun was served like a meal, nursed by the sky itself, and superbly nourished by the two of them.[3]

4

The Idea in the Being of Things

. . . the tree that may be thinking things within.
—Rainer Maria Rilke

B EING, THE ENERGY INTERNAL to things. The energy that thrusts them without, toward the light. The story of the tree that, in its prison, seeks the sun to the point of bursting through an attic window is a powerful illustration.

The reader will have noticed that, in order to evoke the mystery of being in things, we have until now appealed to examples drawn from the world of flora. This is the case, once more, with Rilke's question, in contemplating a walnut tree in front of his Swiss chateau, whether "the tree may be thinking things within." And it is true that, in the course of their formation, plants and animals seem to be inhabited by an intelligent organizing principle, recalling, by analogy, the *idea* of the artist.

Aristotle, reflecting on the generation of living beings, had the same impression. He was led by his numerous and meticulous experiments to speak of the *eidos*—the "idea," let us say—that presides over the genesis of living beings. He explains his insight with the following formulation: "If we fashion a thing, it is produced by nature; and if nature produces a thing, it is fashioned by us" (*Physics* 2.8; 199a3). In *The Parts of Animals,* Aristotle speaks of an "ingenious nature," and an "organizing and creative nature."

After this, how can we refuse to admit that a "reason" penetrates the energy that the entity expends in its formation! Even before Aristotle, Heraclitus of Ephesus (sixth century B.C.) used the word *logos,* which means "reason." Moreover, according to him, philosophy consists in this single task: "to know the *logos* that permeates everything everywhere."[4] He spoke in this way because he was so struck by the regularity with which living beings pursued their formation, from seeds or embryos to maturity.

We readily see how close these first thinkers of nature are to the great biologist Claude Bernard (1813–1878). A renowned embryologist, champion of the experimental method, Bernard admitted that he was unable, in his explanations, to do without what he called the "directive idea of things":

> In a living seed, there is a creative idea, developed and manifested by organization. Throughout its existence, the living organism remains under the influence of this same vital, creative force; when this force can no longer act, death occurs. Here, as everywhere, everything derives from the idea, which alone creates and directs.[5]

We can conclude, then, that it is in the living creatures of nature, in the travail of genesis, that the life force clearly reveals the presence of an immaterial principle, independent of physical, chemical phenomena. This principle can accurately be termed a "creative idea." However, we must always specify that we are not talking about an "idea" in the sense of knowing. This idea is not a similitude of the thing in the human mind. It is an idea that makes something to be, like the idea of David or of Moses in the sculptures of Michelangelo. In examining the paths that these natural beings follow at the moment of their appearance, we are persuaded to reverse the proverb and say, "Nature imitates art"—with this exception: in natural organisms, the creative impulse originates from within themselves.

Here is how a contemplative monk communed with the wisdom found in nature: "The beeches reveal a wonderful script, and I participate devoutly in their autumnal changes. Then there are the maples, which shed their leaves rather quickly after having burst into a fantastic flame. What wisdom there is in these phenomena, these rhythms!"[6]

5

Matter Takes Form

Cézanne seeks to paint matter in the process of giving itself form.

—M. Merleau-Ponty

SURELY THE READER has seen by now that the numerous terms invented by the Greek thinkers, from Thales to Aristotle, refer to one reality alone: *being*. But precisely because the act of being, the object of their investigations, offers such a wealth of intelligibility, a great number of concepts, and thus of words, are necessary to express it.

The term "idea" (*eidos*), to which we were introduced in the foregoing chapter, indicates being as an intelligible principle in all things. Along with this term, Plato (428–348 B.C.), and Aristotle after him, used yet another expression: "form" (*morphē*). The prodigious combat between these two philosophers took place over this term, of which struggle Goethe said that the two of them forever divided up between them the whole universe of thought.

Plato had also perceived that the things of nature in their development appeared to be directed by their "ideas." But he could not think that these ideas, in their stability, could work

16

immediately on matter, which was always changeable. To him, a union did not appear possible between the ideas and the matter that dispersed being and that was therefore responsible for death. Plato was led to say, in this regard, that in nature there were only deficient and evanescent copies of models that dwelt in their perfection only in another world. In Raphael's painting *The School of Athens,* Plato points his finger majestically to heaven. The philosopher's observation must not stop here below. The philosopher's homeland, his and her residence, is the intelligible heaven.

Aristotle, on the other hand, defends the world here below. He understands that we cannot deprive matter of its place in reality. But he did first examine Plato's "ideas" at length when he was meticulously studying hundreds of living species, as he reports in his *History of Animals.* A certitude then struck him. The idea, this principle of vital evolution from the seed to the point of its birth, actually works immediately within matter. So many times had he followed its organizing and shaping power. He had seen it at work in bodies. He could no longer admit that these bodies were only copies or images. The intelligent effort of this matter-in-genesis actually deserved the name of reality.

Having so often reflected on the formative work accomplished by being in its thrust toward the light, Aristotle called being "form," as well. Being is form in matter. Aristotle sought to bring to the forefront precisely the structuring power of unity found in the "idea." He wished to speak not of the external form of bodies, but of their inner texture, which seals the parts into a cohesive whole.

Aristotle has given his name to the teaching that puts an end to the conflict between idea and matter. In fact, his doctrine is called "hylemorphism"—a word constructed from *hylē,* which means "matter," and *morphē,* meaning "form." What Aristotle meant is that matter is not opposed to the formative

and creative idea. On the contrary, in a certain sense matter
calls for it. Aristotle has celebrated the fact that matter has a
vocation for being. For this reason, he gives a special place in
his explanations to the analogy of art. The unhewn marble
waits for the form of the statue. When this form comes, the
sculptor will somehow draw it out from the marble. Thus, in
Michelangelo's *Prigionneri* we witness the rough-hewn "pris-
oners'" attempt to free their limbs from the stone. A rough-
hewn sculpture enables us to see better than anything else that
sculptors do not find their forms outside of matter, but rather
in it, where these forms are in a state of being-able-to-be—of
having the potentiality to become being. Michelangelo liked to
repeat what his teacher Bertoldo used to say: that the sculptor
had to "take out" the statues from the marble. And he added:
"Each block of marble contains hundreds of forms in potentiality. Otherwise, all sculptors, having the same block, would
create identical works."[7]

What fascinates us in Cézanne, Soutine, or van Gogh is that
we witness the effort of form to come immediately to matter,
where the two will at last live on—live, from their union, with
the form communicating its light to matter, its receptacle. For
Cézanne, art is a "little piece of nature."[8] For him, all matter is
still trembling with the fact that, in it, form comes to light.

With certain painters and sculptors, we have the impression
that the form has been imposed upon the matter, introduced
from without. This is especially obvious in the art of the Acad-
emy. Pictorial and sculptural beauty truly exists only when the
form springs from the matter. The painter and the sculptor
create beauty when they *draw* the form from the depths. And
just at the moment when the forms come to birth, they pour
out on matter a light that irradiates it.

We see this in Chagall's painting *The Chariot.* The circle of
the wheels trembles at not being able—fortunately—to meet the
demands of geometry. The case is similar with van Gogh,

where we find uncertain contours in his representation of a chair. With Soutine we find the vacillating lines of trees and houses. This is not naiveté, such as we find in the art of children. Rather it is a poignant witness to a unique moment: when the human creator calls upon a form to come, to emerge, to appear in the light–but once more, to come, to emerge, from the night of matter.

6

The Completion of Being in Things

The living being does not go forth entirely from its causes. It also goes toward them.

—Gabriel Germain

THE THINGS OF NATURE still have secrets to reveal to the philosopher and the poet. What astonishes them both is that the energy that thrusts things into being is found to be directed, aimed toward an end, fin-alized. Thus, Rainer Maria Rilke (1875–1926) admires the kind of haste that seizes the fig tree in the course of its growth. It eliminates everything that could slow it in the production of its fruit. The sixth of his *Duino Elegies* begins:

> Fig tree, for a long time this has been a sign to me,
> that you almost entirely bypass blossoms
> and press your pure secret,
> without ostentation, in the early-chosen fruit.[9]

Depending on their species, individual bodies go their way without fail, following different routes toward their specific ends. Being bursts forth in joyous cries in the bird that leaves its nest. It lavishes itself in colors and fragrances in the flower newly opened, and in the flavor of the fruit. Aristotle much admired this happily victorious impulse. He even invented a term to describe it: *entelechy*. What he wanted us to see by means of this term was the fact that living organisms operate *in* themselves, *upon* themselves, and *for* themselves. Etymologically speaking—in terms of the original meaning of the syllables—the word "en-tel-echy" means "in-end-having": that which "has its end in itself." The word expresses the thrust of something in search of its own realization.

When the plant has begun to flower, when the tree has borne its fruit, they stop. The energy expended until this moment, increasing their being, they now use simply to maintain themselves. This "will" to last, to abide, shows us very clearly that they have been seeking their realization. Here is their good, their glory! "See this rose, in which being is manifested at the pinnacle of its presence!"[10]

In order to *be*, the living being assimilates some of the substances of the outer world by the act of nutrition. But this activity also implies a power of exclusion, which rejects, pushes away all that would compromise life. In its creations, nature performs operations comparable to those of the artist. It chooses—that is, it assimilates and eliminates. Michelangelo called sculpture *la forza de levare*—the "power to raise" from a block of marble whatever prevents the form present there from emerging. Thus, nature in the seed or embryo endeavors to attain new being, while eliminating everything in its path that could make it deviate from that path.

This directive force, this inner call—"finality"—represents another aspect of being in natural bodies. Again, Rilke has wonderfully extolled the patient effort of a walnut tree, in whose shade he loves to linger. He praises the tree for knowing how to repel the forces that could have interfered with the development of its form.

A tree, that comes to self-mastery
by slowly conferring on itself
the form that eliminates
the hazards of the wind.[11]

7

Substance:
At the Roots of Being

In the flower,
there is a within,
that opens its eyes,
and unveils, ever more profoundly,
a form that ravishes
by its proportions and its hues.

—Hans Urs von Balthasar

B EING—THAT IS, THE ACT that thrusts things to stand fast in themselves, from a point of departure in the matter in which this act works—has been given yet another name. Certain philosophers refer to it as "substance."

Why this name? In thus signifying being in yet another way, we can resolve a contradiction that things seem to contain.

On the one hand, in nature things appear as a continuous flux, with multiple and changing aspects. In the sixth century B.C., Heraclitus of Ephesus compared reality to the ceaseless flow of a river. We can think of a rose, and the many stages through which it passes. Hidden in the form of a seed, it subsequently appears as a bud. Then it blossoms. And between these quite different moments, it does nothing but change. Similarly, on the curve of human life, we note the stages of embryo, infancy, adolescence, adulthood, and finally old age. At each of these stages, we could easily think that we were in the presence of a different being!

However, at the source of this succession of states so diverse and so numerous, this almost contradictory succession of modes of being, a nucleus resists, a center remains unchanged. Otherwise, would it be correct to call this ensemble-in-motion by a single name, such as "rose," or "human being"? No matter at what point we encounter them in their development, we surely feel that it is correct to give them a single name.

We can now do a bit of grammar. The name we give to something for as long as it exists we call a "noun," or "substantive." The latter term is made up of a prefix *sub-*, which means "under," and a root *-stant-*, which means "standing." Thus we have a word that means "standing under" all of the changes that the thing in question undergoes, itself undergoing no change. Now we also have the etymology of the word "substance." A substance is "that which is capable of standing fast," permanent, durable, identical with itself "under" the various modifications it may superficially undergo. "Substance" indicates what remains unchanged in the thing that changes. It represents the *inner* solidity of a thing.

But is it not significant that many other words come to be added to the substantive? We call them "adjectives," because these other words are "thrown-to" ("*ad-ject-*"), thrown against, the substantive, as modifiers. Adjectives are names that are appended to the substantive because the modifications that they denote do not have the power to hold fast in themselves. They depend on the substance in order to exist. Substance—we can call it "the underlying"—lends them the power to hold fast nonetheless.

What can we conclude from this? That there are actually an interior and an exterior in things. The radiant figure of the rose both hides and reveals a mysterious part of itself without which what charms us would never even come to light. What the rose offers us, its color and light, its fragrance, the arrangement of its petals—which we describe with adjectives—

the philosopher calls "phenomena." "Phenomenon" comes from the Greek word *phainesthai*, "to appear," which in turn derives from an Indo-European word for "gleam," "give light." What comes to the light of day emerges from the night of its origin, where the secret of being lies. As Rilke puts it: "You, darkness, clasp everything tightly to yourself!"[12]

Moreover, we can now understand why the faculty whose property it is to know this "interior," this substance, is called "intelligence." The word "intelligence" comes from two Latin words: *intus*, which means "within," and *legere*, which means "to read." The human being is endowed with the ability to "read within" things, to read the intimate interior, the secret of things. To the senses, on the other hand, is given the ability to record "phenomena"—what appears, what gleams in the light.

This analysis of language surely shows that there is accord between the data of common sense and the truths held by the philosopher of being. When the ordinary person speaks of "thing," the metaphysician says "substance." When the former speaks of "aspects," the latter says "accidents" (*ac-*, "to," and *-cid-*, "fall"—modifications "falling to" substance). Nevertheless, we see that the mystery of being that the philosopher strives to disclose, in an invented language, is already hidden at the basis of ordinary language.

To be sure, being is substance: a rose. But accidents are being too: the redness, the scent, the height of the rose are real too. What obliges us to call being substance is the fact that *on it* depends all that is captured by the senses—all of its accidents. Let the accidents change or disappear—the color, the scent, the height of the rose—and the rose, the substance, the underlying being of the rose, remains. The rose, the substance, is being-in-itself. The color and so on—the accidents—are being-in-another, being-in-substance. Beyond all of the richness of phenomena, a richness so precious but transitory, are found the hidden roots that nourish the visible, "sensible" order.

It is the particular gift of metaphysician and poet alike to perceive in things, precisely because of what they proffer to be seen, the greater part of their being—an invisible part—that the metaphysician calls their "substance," and the poet their "soul":

> The dead tree—stretched out on tiles of moss,
> victim patient and without anger,
> remains of a prodigious living thing,
> whose soul was so gentle—
> rests in its ample robe of green and russet.[13]

8

The Soul: At the Fountainhead of Being

I have a new hope of doing something, myself, that would have some soul.

—Vincent van Gogh

IN ANTIQUITY ITSELF, and even more so in modern times, philosophers have refused to accept Aristotle's teaching on substance. How, they object, can we postulate an immobile, inert cause as the reason for the being of the incessant flux of phenomena, and of innumerable and changing activities? One might as well try to make life, pure spontaneity, emerge from death!

But this is to bring false charges against Aristotle. If Aristotle called being the "substance" of things, this was because he was seeking to account for the unity and the identity that things retain over time. On the other hand, when he wanted to account for the direction of the activities performed—of the mutations undergone by these same things—he spoke of being as "soul." The soul, as the principle of life, is understood as defining this role of source. For when all is said and done, it is from the very being of things that the flux of phenomena, of successive states, of innumerable activities, springs forth.

Here we must observe at once that, for the ancient philosophers, "soul" did not mean first of all a spiritual principle, separate from matter. No, soul indicates the principle that operates directly on matter, in it, and with it, in order to form the plant, the animal, the person. Later, the soul instills life in the organs, and with them confers on the individual being its specific powers of acting.

When Aristotle was seeking a way to show how the soul is the principle of immanent life, life seated within, he used a comparison, since become classic, between art and nature. Nature "works in living forms." In order to emphasize what belongs solely to the work of the soul, he contrasted it with art. By art, a hand, a torso, a head, can well be created, but these are all dead forms, still life. In speaking of still life, one can say: "To speak of a hand or some other part of the living body to designate aesthetic works makes for an equivocation. This hand will never be able to fulfill its purpose, any more than flutes in sculpture, or a physician in a painting, will be able to fulfill theirs" (*On the Parts of Animals* 1.1; 640b36–641a2).

Once more, these reflections can set in relief the vital powers of nature's being, of the soul responsible for that being. But Aristotle's comparison ought not to obscure the fact that all great artists are rightly obsessed with imparting to their works the intensity of life! What Aristotle has to say does not exhaust the whole truth of art. More than others, the artist feels the soul of things and strives to ensure that whatever exists in things may also abide in his or her works. "When one wants to draw a tufted willow as if it were a living being, and of course it is," wrote van Gogh, "everything that surrounds it simply becomes homogeneous, provided one has concentrated all of one's attention on the tree in question and does not stop until one has made it live."[14] True, it is by means of art that the artist makes it live, but the artist does make it live! The slavish imitation of a plant, an animal, a human being, is not a work of art. Nothing is worse, thinks van Gogh, than the "Academic style," which he calls a "terrible exactitude." And Cézanne, in turn, said, of the same academicism, "the finished work assures the admiration of imbeciles."

The artist of genius is precisely the one who succeeds in investing a hand of bronze, or a marble torso, with life. It has been said of Rembrandt that he is the one who paints "soul." This means the soul of things. From this point of view, nothing is actually more important than his drawings. Has Rembrandt an equal when it comes to capturing in a sketch an animal, a tree, a landscape? The enormous austerity of means contributes only to enhance the radiation of the beauty that the object conceals. The flash of a stroke that seeks, it seems, only to outline quickly the structure (and by what magic?), makes the hidden life of being, its living substance and its soul, stand out!

When van Gogh adds that modern artists "are perhaps the greatest thinkers," he does not mean that they are philosophers. But he announces that there is a kinship between the painter and the philosopher: both need to transcend mere appearances. The artist and the philosopher both know that the secret of things does not reside in what they see. Artist and philosopher alike follow their respective ways to reach the soul of things, which both strive to do. Modern painters, then, more than the ancients, in order to extract from things their spiritual component, persevere against all appearances, which they deform, turn into geometry, and render abstract.

Yes, there resides in things—the philosopher of being knows it, sees it—behind and beyond their appearances, the secret of their substance and their soul. The effort of the artist to "capture" this secret, the conflict that leads to this end, from which the artist always emerges defeated, ought to constitute for the philosopher a stimulating witness to the reality of another world.

We see it, then. To say that the soul is substance is to place it at the most profound center of being. When Aristotle calls the soul "substance" (*On the Parts of Animals* 1.1; 641a25), he means that it is precisely from a point of departure in its being that the living plant or animal develops its organs and fills them with its breath, just as the inspiration of the artist passes through the movements of the arm, the hand, in order to direct the brush or chisel.

9

Philosophers Strive to Translate the Language of Things

Things, and they alone, speak to me.
                                        —Rainer Maria Rilke

SINCE THEY WERE THE FIRST philosophers, the pre-Socratics of the seventh and sixth centuries B.C. received their teachings neither from books nor from persons. It was primarily things that spoke to them. If, up until now, we have been listening especially to Aristotle (fourth century B.C.), that is because he represents a compendium of the history of the first two centuries of philosophy. For his own part, he literally dedicated himself to the study of the beings of nature. In fact, "things" became his primary allusion and reference, even his ultimate one. He liked to say that things do not deceive, and that, if there is an error, it has come from the human mind. And that occurred when the human being did not know how to conform the mind to the real. As has rightly been said, there is, with Aristotle, a "foregone conclusion in favor of things."[15]

Aristotle remarked that, with the first philosophers, as well as with himself, the question is always: What is it to *be*? (*Meta.*

31

7.1; 1028b4). Above every other aspect of being, what captivated their mind was the first act, the universal act, thanks to
which all things come to the light of day and remain there. To
be sure, everyone recognizes this act. But only philosophers
have the gift of making it the object of their astonished
inquiry. This is what our foregoing chapters have been
intended to illustrate. Now let us go back, to summarize the
replies they contain.

We observe that we have needed no fewer than seven words
to denote the intelligible content proper to "being." We have
enunciated these seven names in a certain order, as each of
them clarifies the one coming before it. We need not be surprised at this number of terms. St. Thomas Aquinas explains
it for us: "If one and the same thing bears several names, it is
due to the multiplicity of its properties, or to its multiple
effects" (*Summa Theologica* III, q. 73, a. 4, ad 1). Our summary
intends to show that all of these names are necessary in order
to describe the meaning of natural being. By evincing con-
nections and their necessity, we are opening the way leading
to the philosophical contemplation of things.

In calling those things placed before their eyes "being," the
first philosophers meant that the first act performed by these
things consisted in subsisting by themselves, opposing the
forces of dissolution, defending their own integrity, and when
necessary, restoring the latter.

Cognizant of its origin, philosophers recognized this act as
the thrust that things exert at the heart of their existence. For
this reason, they had to invent a word—*physis*. This word is
untranslatable unless we appeal to the image it contains.
Being, then, is an unfolding toward the light of day: "that
which enters into the light by expanding."[16] The Greek word
physis is akin to *phōs*, which means "light."

But there is more. This internal operation reveals an organizing power. In their growth, plants and animals are strength-

ened with organs adapted for future activities. In order to render these organs functional, living beings unify these instruments, thereby creating autonomous wholes. Accordingly, being also appeared to the early philosophers as constituted by an *idea* (*eidos,* in Greek). But as we have seen, what is really meant is a "visible, governing idea."

Explaining the role played by this governing "idea," Aristotle will emphasize how it arranges the parts of the body, structuring it and forming it. And so he at times called being by the name of *form*—in Greek, *morphē.* But the reader must not think that it is the outward contours of the body that is meant by this term. Rather, it refers to the "architectural" energy dwelling within the being.

Aristotle was first of all a naturalist. He studied living beings by the experimental method. Looking at the work of internal organization effected by the plant and the animal, he much admired the way in which nature directed its work—how nature orders its work toward a purpose. In order to express this, he coined the noun *entelechy,* a name still used by biologists today. It too comes from Greek and denotes whatever possesses its purpose within it. Aristotle observed that, once it has attained its appointed state, being ceases to expand and just "stays put." Being is now established, for it has found its proper good, its own purpose for being.

Then, going back down to the basis of the thing, in admiration at how being, in the long course of this work, with its various aspects—how does it keep its identity and unity?—Aristotle will define being as *substance.* This word signifies being in its function of root of all of the actions the thing performs. This "something" assures us that a rose, or a swallow, deserves to bear the same name—"rose," or "swallow"—from the beginning to the end of its existence.

Finally, we must grant substance, this permanent and hidden ground of being, still another name—*soul.* "The cause of being for all things is its formal substance; but living is for living beings their very *being;* and the cause and principle behind them is the *soul*" (*On the Soul* 2.4; 415b13–14).

Soul, then, is being or substance in living things. Only with living beings does the "idea" or the "form" organize the body by providing it with organs. Into these organs substance infuses the dynamics we call life. It animates these various, specific organs with diverse activities, such as local motion, nutrition, growth, reproduction, sensation, imagination, and memory. By reason of this "animation"—ensoulment—of the body and of the instruments created by it, the substantial form is called "soul."

As the chapters summarized here unfolded the mystery of things, we sought to integrate into these chapters "sayings" of the poets. The quotations cited have conveyed to us the idea that poets too are attracted, like the bee to the flower, by what in the things of nature is the most profound, most hidden, and most substantial.

Unintentionally, our citations, for the most part, refer to a tree, in which, one day, there bursts forth for the poet a shaft of intelligible light. We have said, "*a* tree." The poet is attracted to the individual being—just as one is attached to a person. Ramuz observes it: "Through a single being, *intimately* attained, the poet communes for an instant with all beings."[17] And Rilke: "O tree that may be thinking things within. . . ."

As we gather these quotations, as we concentrate on them, we are persuaded that the poet and the metaphysician feed on the same mystery, on one and the same intelligibility, of which they go in search at the very depths of the real. We must say the same of the painter. Van Gogh said: "I see in my work an echo of what has struck me. I see that nature has told me something, has spoken to me, and that I have taken it down in stenography."[18]

And thus we observe that beginners can encounter the

metaphysical truth of things. If the way of technical language is impractical for them, the way of poetry is available for their consolation. A great poet, Saint-John Perse, has extolled the two ways open to us as we seek for what is most profound:

> Of discursive thought or poetic contractions, which goes farther, and returns from farther? And from this original night where two persons blind from birth grope their way, the one equipped with scientific apparatus, the other helped only by flashes of intuition, who returns the sooner, laden with a brief phosphorescence? The answer does not really matter.[19]

We can also pose the question: *Which of the two goes highest?* Jacques Maritain once observed, with humor: The poet and the metaphysician "play on a see-saw, taking turns rising up to the sky. The spectators make fun of the sport; but they are seated on the ground."[20]

In our next chapter, we shall watch the two as they mount skyward!

10

Discovery of the
Intelligent First Cause

You are a fish, of the great depths,
luminous and blind. . . .
You rise when you please,
from where you please.
You rise not by machine.
You rise like a cork
toward the regions that require you.
                    —Jean Cocteau to Jacques Maritain

To the philosophers, the being of things has revealed its depths. In doing so, it has led them on to discover another being, which hides its mystery beyond our perceptions. Like a cork, they have risen to the sphere where being is distinct from matter. Indeed, from the very beginning the Greek thinkers claimed that with prime matter, working in it or with it, there is a spiritual principle. They called it "spirit," or "reason," even "intellect."

The very first philosopher, Thales (500 B.C.), has left us, in one or two fragments of his works, a testimonial on the subject of this spiritual principle. Thales is known for having posited that, at the origin of all things, is water. For him, water represented an eternal substance, whence, by metamorphosis, have emerged the various bodies of nature. But he added that this substance was "full of spirits," and that "the elemental moist is penetrated by the divine power that sets it in motion."[21] In this way, then, a divine energy oversees the birth of things!

A century later, Heraclitus compared reality to a river, because things never cease to change, in an uninterrupted flow. No less insistently, however, he claimed that a *logos,* in other words a "reason," inhabits this flux. He saw that the process of nature is directed: he saw at work the laws of dialectics, driving matter. For Heraclitus, philosophy lies principally in knowing this reason. "There exists but a single wisdom: to know the thought [*logos*] that guides all things through all."[22]

We must await Anaxagoras of Clazomenae (fifth century B.C.), however, to see prime matter distinguished from the principle that informs it. Anaxagoras calls the latter *nous,* that is, "mind," "spirit." He gives us this description: "Of all things, mind is the lightest and purest. It possesses every kind of knowledge of everything, and the greatest strength. It is infinite, free, one in and by itself." Furthermore, he explains why he posits this intelligent efficient cause: it is the arrangements, the structures donned by matter, prime matter, that "demand" the presence and the labor of mind or spirit in matter. "Whatever there now is," he said, "it is mind [or spirit] that has ordered them."[23]

Anaxagoras received Aristotle's enthusiastic approval. Aristotle declared Anaxagoras to be the only enlightened philosopher among the Greek thinkers before Socrates (late fifth century B.C.). "When you find a person saying that there is an intelligence at work in nature, the cause of the universal order and arrangement, it is like finding a single sober person amidst a gang of drunks" (*Meta.* 1.3; 984b14–17).

We must say that Aristotle's experimental studies, dealing with all sorts of plants and animals, led him to the same conclusion. More than once, he enjoyed the work of the "ideas," of the "forms," at the heart of matter. He differed from Plato in that he recognized, in the matter that he was studying, the intelligent work of nature when it constructed its works of architecture. One day, in his tractate called *On the Parts of*

Animals, he stopped his explanation in order to address a hymn of wonder to this "mind":

> To tell the truth, certain of these creatures do not present a charming sight. Still, the knowledge of nature's plan in them assigns to those who can grasp causes, the truly authentic philosophers, some ineffable delights. Truly, it would be unreasonable, and absurd, that we should find pleasure in contemplating the [artistic] images of these beings because we appreciate at the same time the talent of the sculptor and the artist, and that, in examining these creatures in themselves, in their organization by nature, we would not experience a pleasure even greater than that aesthetic contemplation, provided that we could grasp the intercalation of causes. We need not yield, then, to a childish repugnance that would deter us from the examination of the least of these animals. In all parts of nature, marvels exist.
>
> It is said that Heraclitus, found warming himself by the kitchen fire, called to some visitors who hesitated to enter, "Come in! There are gods in the kitchen, too!" Similarly, then, we should enter without any distaste upon the study of every kind of animal. In each we shall find nature, yes, and beauty. It is not chance, but finality which regulates the works of nature, and this to a high degree. But the finality that directs the composition or the productions of a being is precisely what gives rise to beauty. (*On the Parts of Animals* 1.5; 645a7–25)

Thus, experimentation and demonstration have required of Aristotle that he ascend all the way to an explicit recognition of the active presence of an intelligence in nature. We shall hear him again when he tells us why this intelligence is separated from matter. "To ascribe to matter" and chance "such a beautiful work is not reasonable." The first stage of philosophical intelligence has been first of all to distinguish these two principles of things: matter and mind. Then, gradually, Aristotle establishes the transcendence of mind over matter.

11

Discovery of Pure Act

When we think of God,
and meditate on God,
we have need
neither of our eyes,
nor of our ears,
but we have as guide
the idea of "cause."

—Paul Claudel

TO ADMIRE THE STRUCTURES that nature spreads before our gaze, and to recognize there the signature of the first intelligence, is the privilege of the philosopher. But it is not only "this light architecture, made for soaring," that ravishes the philosopher in the contemplation of the "nautical contours" of the bird. The philosopher also wonders about the thrust that snatches it from the ground and seeks to understand whence it has the secret strength that severs "the thread of its gravitation."[24]

Being is not solely that energy that draws a body from the bosom of matter, to build it up in itself. When it comes into the world, being shows that it is inhabited by tendencies, spontaneous inclinations to act. To be a rosebush is to be impulse to blossom. To be a bird is to be ready for flight, like an arrow in a bent bow. To be a human being is to be desire for knowledge. These needs of act pertain to substances. And now the

39

domain of acting, as vast as that of being, invites the philosopher to descend one more time into its depths.

Every "agent"—anything that acts—here below, before exercising its specific actions (the rose in blooming, the bird in flying, the human being in thinking) is first "in potency" to its acts. Could it find in itself alone the cause of its "going into action"? Compared to the power to act, action is evidently more. It is, once more, in being. To think is more than to be able to think. But however deep one may delve into a power to act, one shall not be able to find there the power to pass over to action. In every power, in every faculty, and in the being possessing them, there will always be a "radical poverty." There must "intervene"—there must enter within this power, these faculties—a thrust whose source will always remain mysterious.

Aristotle is the first of the Greek thinkers to declare that the action and movement of individual natural agents have their first explanation in the enveloping motion of a transcendent, universal agent. He calls that agent *first substance, pure act* (*Meta.* 12.7; 1072a23–25).

He adds that this universal agent, *pure energy,* could not be found at the level of things. Since it actuates, activates, all natural agents, and each one individually, it must be independent of them. We are moved to read this pagan, as he says: "There must be a first mover. It must not be under the dependency of another. For it is the agent responsible for all of the actions and movements of subordinate substances" (*Physics* 8.5; 256a19–21).

This source is hidden. Never will the senses be able to seize it. The intelligence alone obliges us—on pain of falling into absurdity—to posit it, in order to give an account of this *more* represented by action in relation to a being that is as yet only in potency to acting. For its part, this universal agent must not be the subject of any change. "Immobile, it is ever the strength to move all things, eternally" (*Physics* 8.10; 267b3–5).

While recourse must be had to a certain logical rigor in order to establish the presence of this pure act, there is a tenderness in its recognition, as well. A theologian, who is also a poet and a metaphysician, says this in terms of great delicacy:

> It is a strange mystery, this presence of God at the very heart of the energies of the universe, in order to raise them from their potency. A blade of grass bent by the wind, a twinkling star, a lovely scent spreading abroad, a beating pulse—nothing of this would be possible without the secret, constant motion of God. If—although it would be impossible—this motion were to suspend its influx, the universe would be instantly immobilized—would fix, would petrify, would change into an unimaginable residue of dead substances. All sighing, all life, all cry, all desire, all thought, all love, would be forthwith extinguished.[25]

A passage like this permits us to discern how a great metaphysics and the Gospel are destined to merge their respective lights. The doctrine of pure act—thus presented—must, as we see, await the revelation of Christ in order to keep all of its promises. It is the Gospel, of course, that will open to our gaze the lilies of the fields, the birds of the air, enveloped by the gentle providence of the Father of heaven, who sustains them, clothes them, feeds them. The medievals were not wrong, then, to place at the portals of their cathedrals the statue of Aristotle bent low: human wisdom, at the feet of the apostles, awaits their demand for its services!

12

Being: Essentially a Desire for God

Does not all creation everywhere show us the initiative belonging to the final cause–that is, belonging to the need that the Creator has judged it well that we should have here in the universe?
—Paul Claudel

METAPHYSICIANS WHO SOUND the depths have still more astonishment in store. Deep down in things, they are about to discover yet another mystery. A more in-depth analysis of action unveils to them another secret. Pure act exerts on natural agents still another form of causality.

A being of nature, as we have seen in our preceding chapter, becomes an "agent" only if its potencies of acting pass into act. For this, a motion must be applied to it. It must be, as it were, thrust to act. But this does not suffice. Besides being invited, it must also be attracted–magnetized, so to speak. A being of nature emerges from itself only if its action brings it a complement, a completion, a desired being-more. At the root of action, there is in the agent a love of its good. To be a bird is to love flight, to be a human being is to love to know. The action is thus for being, for a good–its good.

But we must see that, in an individual thing, the good dons manifold modalities. For example, it is doubtless its good that the bird seeks in nourishment. But it accomplishes this activity also for the good of the species to which it belongs, when it feeds its young. Myriad facts demonstrate that the animal sacrifices itself for the perpetuation of the species. In observing it act, one would say that its great concern, its sole concern, is to save the species from death, to perpetuate it.

And there is more. All species, and each individual, have, besides, another good that they pursue: being. Being: behold the object of the primordial desire in all things. It is because it loves to "be" that this tree expends so much effort to come to the light and stand fast in it.

But from the other direction, we must add at once that, if being belongs to all individuals and to each one, all and each belong to being, as well. Birth and death—are these not indisputable signs that being is a gift to them? Rather, let us say: lent to them. All and each, then, depend on the being that is by and in itself, and which alone is the cause of the being of other things.

Upon this fact of a philosophic order, St. Thomas Aquinas pronounces this principle: "When a being has in another its entire reason for being, it is impossible that it not love, by nature, this other more than itself." And he serenely adds: "Under this aspect every being naturally loves God more than itself" (*STh* I, q. 60, a. 5, ad 1). Here a caution is in order. We must not ascribe to this love for God a psychological, moral character. It is neither conscious nor voluntary. It is part and parcel of the being of all things. It is a natural, necessary love. Still, it is not coerced but spontaneous.

In every individual of nature, then, we distinguish a threefold dynamism. This bird traces lines on the page of heaven because it seeks nourishment for itself, to preserve its individual being. Then it does so also in order to feed its young, and thereby preserve the species. And during all of this time, it is impelled by a primordial, concealed, mysterious desire. Since it receives its being from absolute being, which possesses being by itself, it therefore loves God, pure act. This is what makes Aristotle say: "From this principle hang heaven and nature" (*Meta.* 12.7; 1072a13–14).

Thus, both upstream and downstream from the things of nature, there is being-by-itself: source and end. There is God who moves things to action, and God drawing them at the same time. Here is the double action without which the innumerable universe of beings would remain inert and dead.

> Justice inspires my divine Artisan:
> I was constructed by Omnipotence,
> Supreme Wisdom and First Love.[26]

These lines from Dante sum up the teaching of our last three chapters. Philosophers' regard is drawn first to the depths of the things of this world. And in these depths they discover the traces of three attributes belonging to the being that is not part of the region where being is clothed in matter.

In the act of constructing itself in an architectural form, being manifests the action of a transcendent intelligence. At the same time, the energy that applies being to action and the good that draws it to emerge from itself have their source in the activation of an omnipotent energy, and a first love.

As we see, the philosopher discovers in the depths of things the traces of God. Let us give ear once more to the poet as he testifies to this power of things.

> By what do we recognize a living being that we do not see? By the movement it governs. The mole underground, the hare in the hedgerow, the heart behind the fingers. Now, we see that the whole universe moves. Everything in this world is in movement, and bears witness to the sacred agitation of creatures, ever in a state of creation, incapable of existing by itself, of subsisting, in the presence of an immobile creator. Everything betrays its influx.[27]

13

The Metamorphoses of Bodily Being

*We are in astonishment
at the metamorphoses we have seen to our very day.
It is from the heart of the perfect caterpillar
that the butterfly is born,
everlasting and perfect like it
in its pure novelty.*

—Dom Vermeil

THE BEING OF THINGS, the act that we call being and that is their inmost heart, reveals to the philosopher its mystery. At the same time, it speaks of another being, beyond things but at work in them. It must be said, however, not all has been unveiled of the secret hidden in things. Another part of the mystery of corporeal being, over the last two centuries, has also come to light.

Before the scientist Lamarck (1744–1829), minerals, plants, and animals were accounted as belonging to fixed species. Species presented themselves as fixed categories, into which the things of matter must necessarily enter. A catalogue of these species described in advance the figures, the structures that living beings had to take. Everyone—philosophers also—thought that the botanical and zoological species were nature's "clear and distinct ideas." Some taught that all species were eternal. As for the Bible, it revealed that the creator had set species, with matter, on the earth, in the waters, in the air.

They were fixed, then. This is how theologians and intellectuals, at least most often, interpreted the first page of Genesis.

But little by little, scholars perceived that the botanical and zoological species had a "history," as indeed did the earth itself. They saw that living species had not always existed—that they, too, like their individuals, had been engendered—that certain ones of them had even been extinguished.

This scientific "revelation" of a genesis of species has its origin in sciences that Paul Claudel calls, more correctly, "chronicles": geology and paleontology.[28]

First, geology recounts how the earth has been formed, in a series of transformations that have left different strata. The history of the earth unfolds in four stages: the primary, secondary, tertiary, and quaternary ages. But in the course of creating their inventory of these stages, scientists have found, inscribed in them, precisely another history: that of the botanical and zoological species. This "underground library" contains no papyri, no parchments. It contains fossils of clay and stone. In these pieces of stone and earth, plants and animals have left proofs of their existence. Reduced to pure schematic structures, in the manner of A. Giacometti's (1901–1966) sculptures, these testimonials speak of an evolution of species. They are indeed a "chronicle" of the forms of being. These forms, then, are found in stages, in the various eras—ages of the earth in which they are found—and all together they manifest a genealogy. Geology and paleontology are of one accord in attesting that species are "temporal," and that among them, we find both succession and ascendancy.

These "chronicles" thus evince the reality of natural forms that were once alive. One who visits this "underground museum" sees that these forms were neither contemporary, nor immediately successive. They are similar to the "museum of images of world sculpture," where one could follow the successive styles, from the Venuses of prehistory to the forms of

Moore and Brancusi. Both the evolution of these forms and their filiation are in evidence. André Malraux (b. 1901) has spoken, in their regard, of a "metamorphosis of the gods."

And indeed the "prehistoric museum" of the forms of nature offers the spectacle of the metamorphoses of corporeal being. We are made aware of this by the series of "ideas" that nature has realized in the course of time. But especially, we have proof that these successive "ideas," these successive forms of being, have known a genesis, in the course of time, according to the ages of the earth, and that a bond of similarity and dependency enables us to establish the genealogical tableau.

If we now pass from the simple fact to an explanation of this "transformism," scientists offer various hypotheses. The successive appearance of species and their kinship are, we are told, the results of efforts at adaptation. For example, in order to subsist when being must pass from water to air, through a stage in which they live on dry land, the individuals of a species have "transformed" themselves, for the purpose of being able to respond to new conditions of life: "An ingenious adaptation of its fin suddenly allows the water animal to soar aloft."[29] Paleontologists show us how the form of the bird has emerged from that of reptiles.

All of this shows that we find, in the birth of a species, what we find in the birth of an individual being in an already constituted species. We can distinguish three acts:

First, the new form emerges from a point of departure in the individuals of a previous species. Second, the new form, the origin of a new species, will "hold fast in itself." Third, it checks the forces of destruction by multiplying its individuals by reproduction. The age of species is impressive. Certain species of ants have existed at least thirty million years.

At this point in our reflection, we must pose the question: But what is a species? It is a category that, as such, exists only in the mind. One does not find species in reality, but only its representatives. Species is a logical category. Still, there is something corresponding to it, founding it in reality. We are inclined to speak of the "substantial form" that structures things. There is a "directive idea" organizing the development of individuals. And this "idea" abides in countless individuals.

We grasp, then, that, on the philosophical plane, the evolution of species is reducible to the question of the origin of substantial forms, the origin of these "ideas of nature" consisting in these forms. Thus, paleontology and geology oblige the philosopher to take up once more the question of the origin of species: since they are not eternal, since they come from one another by a genealogical path, how are we to represent to ourselves this lengthy becoming of the forms of being in the history of nature?

The response that the philosopher of "being" is led to make to this question causes us still more admiration of the "style of the Creator."

14

The Play of Matter and the Divine Artist

God has not made the world,
he has made it make itself.
He has provoked it.

—Paul Claudel

THE EVOLUTIONARY VIEW of the forms of being in nature is founded on numerous facts. Paleontologists have evinced the succession of forms and their ascendant movement over the course of billions of years.

But the massive fact of evolution poses a serious problem to philosophers of being. They wonder whether they must hold that new, more perfect, being comes from antecedent, less perfect being. Can more come from less? Philosophers cannot escape this question. They must neither deny the facts, nor try to explain them with absurdities. And so they ask: Is it possible that forms—these "ideas" of nature—find their sufficient cause in matter alone? For example, does one have the right to say with the evolutionist: "Life is born of matter—indeed, non-living matter"?[30]

The first quality we hope to meet in the philosopher who seeks to respond to this question is a sense of mystery. Philosophers interrogate the sources, which always are secret. First

49

and foremost, they should experience the mystery hidden in original matter, the matter-matrix whence come the forms. All matter conceals limitless potentialities. As we know, Michelangelo loved to repeat the maxim of his teacher, Bertoldo: "Every block of marble contains, in potency, hundreds of forms; otherwise would sculptors not have to make identical works from the same marble?"[31] Or who would have thought, before seeing them, that rock could contain so many forms, as we see them in the "museum of images"?

It is essential, in order to shed light on this question of origins, to see that the matter from which nature extracts its works is analogous to the matter from which art draws its own works. The plasticity of the former, however, wins the day. That contemplative monk was right who remarked on the subject of matter: "We can forbid these depths nothing. Can we be surprised at the metamorphoses that we are still seeing?"[32] In order to reply to this question, we must become sensitive to the limitless ductility addressed by the divine artist.

The divine artist, as we call this being, enjoys a privilege here. The divine artist has the power of producing, independently of other causes, the matter from which future forms are to be drawn. And precisely the evolution of these forms, their manifold apparition, advises us that the matter at the disposition of the divine artist is so indeterminate at the outset as to forbid this being nothing from then on.

There is more. The matter prepared by the divine artist is not like that on which the human artist works. The matter on which the human artist works is purely passive, pure "awaiting." The matter from which natural forms come to light is, on the contrary, already worked, by a kind of unquenchable desire for all sorts of possible forms. The matter of natural forms possesses, deep within it, a limitless appetite for all of the forms of being.

This "desire," this "appetite," can be explained. Matter comes from the first cause, which is the act of being-as-such. When this cause acts, it tends to engender in being a participation of likenesses of itself. Thus, when matter receives one of the possible forms of being, it retains an "appetite" for others. To the divine artist, matter shows itself rich in an indefinite capacity of forms. Matter is produced to serve as the "subject" of numberless similitudes of perfect being. The divine artist has willed and produced it in order to give "reality" to the innumerable divine "ideas."

Because the divine artist is necessarily intelligent, this artist has produced things in an orderly fashion. Out of infinitely obedient matter, the divine artist has drawn, at first, the forms of the elements. Then other beings, of the mineral order. Then still others, enriching the vegetable and animal orders. Paleontology attests this ordered production. Once this "history of forms" is brought to our attention, we cannot avoid admitting that there is finality here—being operating for an end. We see very well that, in each of these orders, the antecedent forms, besides exercising their own acts, prepare their matter for the emergence of forms still higher in their structure. And we see that these latter, in turn, suppose the former. And thus the whole is a work of intelligence.

But the divine artist also comes forward as the freest and most unforeseeable of inventors. In each of these "orders," the vegetable and the animal, this artist has posited a veritable cascade of the most varied species. To original matter's insatiable "desire" corresponds the indefatigable "invention" of the divine artist. Because that artist is a poet, and because that artist knows from experience all that a creative imagination can inspire, Paul Claudel was able deliciously to evoke the play that the creator engages in with matter. Claudel wrote:

What is deepest in matter is humor, a sense of the mischievous. One would say that Prakriti knows very well that her creator has made her only to have fun with her, even though she pretends not to notice. She upholds her own part very well—she "plays along." And when she is scolded, she closes her eyes, and with an enchanting smile—like a rose as pure as the breath of a girl—exhales a butterfly.[33]

15

The Creator's Style 1

*Sculpture is an art that permits one to withdraw
everything superfluous from the matter lying before
the artist, thereby reducing it to the form sketched
out in that artist's mind.*

—Donatello

ONE CANNOT PLACE the whole *raison d'être* of the evolution of the forms of nature in the aptitude of matter to receive them. A pure can-be, a pure aptitude, even already worked by desire, does not suffice to explain the emergence of new, "more" being. To pass from one perfection, modification, of being to a higher one, there must surely be a capacity on the part of matter to be enriched by the latter. But an agent cause is necessary as well—in other words, a cause capable of producing the higher perfection of being. Matter does not find that in its can-be!

Aristotle is the first philosopher to have compared, in this question, the work of nature to the work of art. He liked to say: "The cause of the building is the materials, surely; but even more it is the building that is in the mind of the architect." He said: "The building comes from the building, the material from the immaterial" (*Meta.* 7.7; 1032b11–12). The building to come is in the materials, but only in potency. In the intelligence of the architect, it is in act, in actuality. For an intelligence sensitive to the demands of being, the evolution of forms therefore calls for two causes: the matter, with its aptitude for forms, and the first intelligence, with its architectural ideas.

Paleontology and geology, in establishing the rise of the specific forms in matter, teach us better to situate the formative and "plasmative" activity of the divine artist. Because this divine artist is spirit or mind, and because this divine artist conceives things, it is in this mind that the "ideas" of things are found. In the divine artist, things transcend matter. But when this artist decides to "real-ize" them, it is within matter that the action of real-ization takes place. The divine artist does not work "on" matter, as if this divine cause were somehow external to it. For a pure spirit, spatial concepts are non-signifying. On the other hand, this artist does not "impose" these ideas on matter—matter is the desire for all forms. As the greatest of all artists, this one brings forth the forms corresponding to the divine ideas from "within" matter itself, matter with its limitless capacity to be shaped and molded.

What is beautiful in God's activity, and in the work of the greatest artists, is that they do not superimpose a form on matter as one forces clay into a ready-made mold. No, the art of both is to invite a form by which the matter becomes intelligible and sensible to the mind.

When the new form thus sought, and as it were called, arrives in the light, it radiates tenderly in the matter to which it is thankful for having been able to traverse its maternal night. Is it not this mystery that is celebrated/extolled by Rilke?

> Darkness of origins
> I love you more than I love the flame
> that circles the world—
> You, darkness, clasp everything tightly to yourself.[34]

And so the being of the things of nature owes a great deal to the original matter from which the forms spring. But these forms owe even more to the first intelligence, which conceives them. In speaking of the activity of this intelligence in the evolution of forms, one can only speak of analogy with the work of the artist. Here we must know how to underscore the resemblances, without omitting to remark the differences. If the human artist draws forms, as it were, from the interior of matter, of wood, of stone, of marble, nevertheless this artist acts *on* the matter—let us say, even *against* it. Michelangelo has defined sculpture: the *forza di levare*—the "power to lift" the superfluous stone from around the form, the figure within. And Michelangelo trimmed with chisels and hammers, sending shots of matter to all sides.

There is nothing of this in the divine acting. If we would evoke the work of God in nature, let us listen to a contemplative monk: "When God awakens a new reality, first, he does not act *on* things, or *against* things—as we are obliged to do. God works *in* them. The new form is conceived at the very *center* of the existing being "from which the new one is to be extracted."[35]

The universe of the forms of nature, according to their succession in time, and their "lineage," speaks, then, once more in favor of the divine agent. But it speaks of a creator who manages the process while hiding the creative power in the depths of things. Who expresses this mystery of a universal intervention and at the same time of an infinite discretion better than the psalmist?

> My bones were not hidden from you
> When I was fashioned in secret,
> Embroidered in the depths of the earth.
> —Psalm 139:15

16

The Creator's Style 2

*Inasmuch as all things have their raison d'être
in serving God, God has mercifully consented to
make use of them.*
—Paul Claudel

THERE IS STILL ANOTHER resemblance between the acting of the divine artist and that of the human artist. Both
have recourse to the service of intermediaries between their
action and the work to be created. The sculptor has need of
tools—hammers and chisels. The painter needs a paintbrush.
The musician needs a piano or a violin. And the divine agent
takes advantage of the energies of structures already existing,
the universal cosmic agents: water, air, light. Thus all nature
collaborates in the work to come. "The creator sees to it that
everything conspires, and from all eternity, in the being now
appearing."[36] Thus, just as with the production of an artifact,
so also the emergence of a new specific form in nature postulates the activation of two efficient causes in synergy.

These two causes belong to two different orders of "efficient" causality. The philosopher defines their rapport by
naming the one "principal cause" and the other "instrumental

cause." Everyone understands, it is true, that the beauty of an engraving of Rembrandt depends first of all on the power of art dwelling in him. But what could he have done without a point? The chemical virtues of the colors employed by Cézanne are not the principal cause of the beauty of his canvasses. But without them, what could he have done? Everything—paintbrush, pigments, movement of the arms, of the hands—shares in the production of the painting. But their own causality finds its place, so to speak, *under* and *in* the maneuvers of the power of art in the painter. This power of art "superelevates" the instruments, "informing" them by virtue of creative intuition, by virtue of the artist's creative idea—and applying them to the work to be created.

Let us return now to the domain of the evolution of species. The doctrine of double causality finds a new point of application here. We shall say, then: The divine artist, the first intelligence, operates, as we have said, at the "center" of all things. It operates by causing a superelevating influx to pass into them. It "super-informs" the action of the universal cosmic agents and the substances involved in the emergence of the new species. A form specifically superior, until now only in potency in the matter, makes its appearance. It is only thanks to the play of this double activation that living species have come from matter.

The specifically superior being is thus the fruit of a collaboration on the part of all nature. The process of genesis of the forms of being depends on the creative intelligence seeing to it that its divine influx passes—without harming them— through natural agents. Through their new agency, natural agents are elevated to the order of instrumental causes of the divine causality. The ascent of specifically superior forms within nature—their genealogical rise over the course of time— recounts the wisdom and power of God as well as (and even better than) a fundamentalist interpretation of the story of creation. And it is correct to say that evolution manifests another "style" of God.

A comparison of the divine acting and the acting of the human artist spares us the necessity of speaking of creation in terms of "fabrication," or "manufacture." One must speak instead of "invention of forms," with all that this term may invoke in terms of groping, seeking, beginning once and then starting over, rough drafts, and—why not come right out and say it—changes of mind. One must be a bit of a poet to under-stand this! Those who have ever read any paleontology can only be delighted to read these humorous lines of Paul Claudel evoking the incredible creative imagination of Prakriti:

> After centuries, and millennia, during which she has set afoot a whole hothouse and a whole menagerie, all of a sudden one would say that she becomes disgusted with it all, is sick of it, sweeps the tray clean with one great backhand, and starts all over. She chucks into the dump whole orders, with their genuses, sub-genuses, and species, keeping only a louse and a cricket.[37]

17

The Creator's Style 3

God has seeded the world to his likeness.
                                                    —Paul Claudel

THE ROLE PLAYED by the first intelligence in the ascending movement of the forms of being in nature is situated in the sphere of "efficiency," agency—*thrusting* causality, the ordinary, prephilosophical meaning of the word "causality." But the direction of this movement that rises toward higher and higher forms implies another form of causality as well, on the part of a divine agent. The progressive evolution of species must be attached, as well, to the *attraction* exercised by the divine good on matter. After all, if the divine agent is intelligence, it is also goodness, and hence "final" cause.

Aristotle had already brought this point out in his explanation of things. He even thought that the mode of causality most applicable to the first cause of beings is not "efficiency," or thrusting cause, but "finality," or drawing cause. He argued, in effect: The first cause of all things, being pure act of being, must be identified with the good, with goodness. The good, too, is being, but inasmuch as it is desired. As the

59

good is that which everything desires, therefore God, who is the *absolute total good*, is the attractive cause of all beings. God operates on them as love does. And he concluded: "Heaven and nature depend on such a principle" (*Meta.* 12.7; 1072b12).

Thus, then, the beings of nature appear among things not only because the pure act of being pushes them but also because it *attracts* them, because it *calls* them to appear. It would not suffice to restrict the appearance of the forms and their evolution only to the divine agent's power of *invention*. They must also be understood as responses to its *invitation*. Evolution should also appear as a "command," says Paul Claudel, made to matter to realize themes from a starting point in its depths. And matter responds with unbelievable fantasy! "When, for example, the theme of the palm, or that of the fern, or that of the mushroom enters the race—its variations are in the tens of thousands!"[38]

There is more. When paleontology and geology have helped one to understand the rise of species, from a point of departure in the most elementary forms of matter all the way up to the human being, one cannot avoid the impression that an immense aspiration pervades these species, and calls them. Surely they are called to breach their boundaries to gain increasing degrees of life, freedom, knowledge, love. At each degree of perfection attained by nature, the history of the transformation of species manifests a tendency to leave it behind and to head onward to a superior form. And this movement ceases only with the human being, who thus appears as the end sought by the rising movement of the forms of nature.

To describe the progressive evolution of species in terms of tendency, aspiration, inscribed in the depths of matter, is to direct one's gaze toward a very mysterious, dark zone of being. To penetrate it will be to discover still another secret of natural being.

But can one discover what it is, within the matter of a corporeal being itself, that creates an expectation, and something like a call to emerge from the limits of its species to attain the perfection of the human form? Yes, if our intelligence will sensitize itself to what makes the most hidden, most fundamental attraction of the being of things. What is this good, then, the most essential one, that a being pursues?

Granted, every being in nature pursues the good of its individuality. This rose, this swallow, each in its own way, protects itself against any agent of destruction threatening it. Here is the proof that its individuality is its most immediate good. But we must likewise notice that each being of nature pursues the good of its species. How often we stand in wonder at how an individual toils to maintain the species. Does not the activity of reproduction, for instance, imply in itself the sacrifice of the individual to the species. How astounding to see the care that an animal takes of its little ones!

But is not that which is the most basic good of a thing more basic than its individuality and its species, its *being*, that is, the act that gives it to hold fast in itself and for itself? Everything loves to *be*. And this love is radical.

Indeed, it is in this love for being that each thing possesses that the tendency and aspiration are found inscribed in each individual to emerge from its species toward a higher degree of perfection. But why? The reason is that in each individual of our world, precisely because of the being it possesses, there is a love for the *being of God* that is still greater than for its own being. St. Thomas Aquinas deciphers this by the following reflection.

> When a being finds in *another all* of the reason for its existence and its goodness, it is impossible that it not love, by nature, this other being more than itself. . . . But God represents a good greater than that of the species. God is the universal Good

purely and simply. Under this rapport, every being naturally
loves God more than itself. (*STh* I, q. 60, a. 5, ad 1)

Is it possible to measure the power of the dynamism that
such a tendency, the most fundamental, the most hidden, the
most unconscious, inserts in the depths of the being of each
thing? But it is very precisely there that one must seek the why
of evolution. It is not at the level of its species that a being of
nature is exercised by the desire of another specific form. It is
precisely on the level of its being. It is there that the tendency
is rooted that carries matter to ever more perfect forms.

Because a being loves God more than itself—and because
this is natural—it necessarily desires, consequently, that the
being of God be "participated" in forms more perfect than its
own. This natural, unconscious desire exercises itself under
the mode of a tendency toward a more perfect degree of
being. And just as, in a being of nature, it is matter that has
the aptitude to receive new forms, it is therefore in matter that
the tendency is found, of which St. Thomas speaks, to receive
the most perfect form.

But in the universe of bodies, in which forms are united to
matter, the highest of forms is the human soul. The human
soul is actually a spirit united to a body, making a single substance with it. But it is a spirit! And St. Thomas concludes:
"Above the human form in the world of generation and cor-
ruption, there is nothing—nothing more perfect. Therefore
the end of all generation is the human soul. Matter *tends
toward it* as toward its last form" (*Summa contra Gentiles* III,
c. 22).

Now we have found the *raison d'être* of the evolution of
species. It is in this tendency, this natural aspiration, consubstantial with the matter of natural being, to pass to degrees of
being more and more elevated. This enormous aspiration per-

meates all species up to the human being. As we see, thus understood, evolution is no stranger to the action of God, because it is inscribed in the being that participates in God.

This process of genesis of forms, wherein nature collaborates with God, who is at once efficient cause and final cause, represents God's "true style."

It takes the genius of Paul Claudel to discover this doctrine in the Bible itself. Commenting on Deuteronomy 4:39 (Vulgate), which says: "The Lord is God in the sky above and on the earth below," Claudel offers a gloss:

> It is therefore himself, above, who calls forth the earth and the water, who furnishes them an idea of what it is that he asks of them, of what he intends to obtain from them, and it is likewise himself below, hidden, who supplies [earth and water] the strength and the matter to be employed, just as it is he who has guided them in the construction of their instruments.[39]

18

Heart of Being,
Hearth of Being

Now, O my God, I know that each thing bears
within itself its mystery, and that you know the
mystery. This is a little flower, and this is a rose.
                                        —Francis Jammes

FROM THE BEGINNING, philosophy has been, and ought always to be, first of all a contemplation of the things of nature. It is under this form that being especially presents itself. Philosophy ought to stop to delve into the being of material things, according to all of the richness that the act of being comports—the act of thrusting out of the night of matter into the light, the act of organizing, building itself into a species. Each thing, indeed, in exercising being, realizes a program: as the rose attains its perfection "in its ardent geometry," as the bird that, "on the page of the sky, is itself the arc and arrow of flight."

And yet the philosopher has not done with being astonished. One day, at the very heart of the propositions in which the intelligence expresses its vision, the philosopher will perceive that there is still "another part" in the being of things. Gerard Manley Hopkins said: "It is only of the hyacinth that is here and now that we can say, 'This *is.*'" He meant that the being of the hyacinth has reality only in an individual plant, which one beholds "in this place" and "now." When I say,

"This is a hyacinth," I bear witness, I assert, that I see in this thing more than the being and its species. I assert that the act of being and the species belong to what I can name only by saying "this." But at all events, I see it as distinct from what I attribute to it.

Let us once more do a bit of grammar, as we have done, in order to understand the meaning of the term "substance." In the expression, "This is a hyacinth," the word "this" is the subject. "This" is the subject of the proposition. What do grammarians mean? They mean that the word "this" is *under* other words. Under the verb "is" and the noun "hyacinth," there is a "this," and to it I "attribute" being, species, and the rest. "Subject" comes from the Latin *sub-jectum*—"cast under."

In this way, it appears to the philosopher's mind that there is something more in a thing than the avowal of its existence, its species, and its attributes. Since the pronominal adjective "this" grounds whatever I attribute to a thing, as "cast under" what I attribute to it, necessarily I designate by "this" the most profound and basic element in the being before me. Thus, in each thing there exists a center, a hearth burning at the heart of being.

On the basis of these reflections, we understand why the philosopher calls this center, this hearth, the "supposit." Etymologically, *sub-posit* means "that which is posited, placed, underneath." Not that one may understand this term as indicating a thing "underneath" another thing. By no means. It only indicates its function in the sentence. As for the reality of the thing, in placing the "this" in this position in the sentence, we clearly see that what it means is "first" in the thing. When I say, "This is a hyacinth," I touch, in the "this," the depth of this thing. I attain, in the thing, its "unique individuality."

What is individual, unique in things it would seem that it is the privilege of the poets to feel. One of them confides: "I make a detour to see again a walnut tree whose presence touches me as if it had been a human face."[40] What touches the poet is not the species of this tree, nor its outward manifestations. Beyond these things is a mystery in it, like that of a person. Another example would be the exclamation of Rainer Maria Rilke in being seized with compassion in the presence of a titmouse that alights on a tree in his garden at Muzot. And he addresses it:

> O you, little heart, who winter
> with us amidst these adversities,
> you alight, little lantern of life,
> on trees in that are in tears.
> I contemplate this fire, that shines
> through your thick plumage.[41]

Unless it leads to a contemplation of this "unique" element residing at the heart of things—or better, constituting the heart of things—philosophy has failed to keep its promises. Indeed, it has blinded its disciple. To be sure, the contemplation of the act of "being" and its interior riches is a precious boon. But this is only one part of the profit that philosophy claims to derive from the real. Although it may be by an altogether other way, the philosopher is also led where the poet goes by instinct: to the individual, the unique, to what is personal and hence ineffable in things.

Neither being, nor the species that being extracts from matter, have their end in themselves. They are ordained, destined, to give birth to, and if possible to give lasting being to, in themselves and by themselves, their respective individuals: this wisp that trembles in the wind this morning; this blade of grass before which I stop because it offers, in the drop of water at its tip, a flash of light. Sometimes, and more profoundly, it is a tree that grasps me to itself like a lover.

> A tree has been my father and my teacher. . . . I have met this tree and I have embraced it. . . . How many afternoons have I passed at its foot, having emptied my thought of all clamor! . . . Now I must find it once more![42]

19

Being Is Concrete Presence

*The idea does not exist. What exists is the
individual.*

—Alain

I T TOOK PHILOSOPHY some time to give the individual its
deserved place at the heart of being—the first place! True,
in terms of being, individual bodies—this flower here—because
of the brevity of their existence, seem not to deserve the
attribute "being." For the first two centuries of philosophy,
approximately, philosophical thought found itself paralyzed by
the aphorisms of Parmenides (515–440 B.C.), a Greek philosopher born at Elea in southern Italy. Parmenides reiterates:
"How could being perish? How could it come to existence?"[43]
In his eyes, birth and death were incompatible with being.
After all, it is the nature of being to be. Therefore individual
things, destined for death, did not have the right, according to
Parmenides, to bear the name of "being." Plato, Parmenides'
brilliant disciple, came to relegate being to another world, in
which matter no longer involved things in the flow of inter-
minable becoming.

Aristotle revolutionized Greek philosophy by insisting on
just the opposite truth, the compendium of his governing intu-

ition: "Only the individual *is.*" What was he seeking to assert? This (an obvious fact, nevertheless): that one meets reality only in individual things. Never does one encounter the species of the hyacinth, or the species of a swallow. One encounters only this hyacinth, this swallow.

But especially, Aristotle has drawn all of the consequences of this fact. He said, "the individual walks at the head of being" (*Ethics* 1.4; 1095b6). He saw that the energy that thrusts the form to be, orders its labor toward the appearance of new individuals in the species. He saw that being, as "act," and the species are at the service of the individual.

In contemplating this fact, we find ourselves before a para-dox! Nothing is as ephemeral as an individual. And yet it is for its sake that being and species toil with all of their strength. Aristotle is right, then: "The individual walks at the head of being." We must conclude, that what is most precious in nature is the individual, which being and species cause to materialize in themselves. The Aristotelian philosopher will understand the poet who is worried about his orchids. Knowing that he was going to die, Rilke sent some orchids to a woman who was a friend of his, with these words: "I should not wish that these orchids would spend their moment of blooming without being the object of anyone's attention. Please give them hospitality."[44]

The paradox that we have just cited looms still larger when we consider that the individual, which is the most precious good in nature, is also the most threatened.

The species, of course, is safe. It maintains itself imper-turbable through the births and deaths of individuals. Some species last for millions of years—certain species of ants, for thirty million years! Compared with numbers like this, what is the lifetime of an ant? When we think of the unique value of a human person, which transcends the good of the entire universe, what a miniscule length of time is represented by her or his passage on this earth!

Individual things die, like this swallow that creases the sky. This one will return no more. And yet Aristotle, against Plato, holds that only the individual has being. It is to it that being is attributed. "It is only of the hyacinth present here and now that we can say: That is." Aristotle saw that it was before his eyes, "in" this flower and "for" it that its specific form was making an effort to thrust itself outside matter and to stand fast in the light.

But individual things die. St. Augustine formulated their enigmatic fate:

> Things are born, and they die. In being born, they begin to be. . . . They grow to attain their perfection, and once they are perfect, they grow old and die. Not everything reaches old age, but everything dies. Thus, when they are born, and *make an effort* to be, the more rapidly they grow to be, the more rapidly they hasten to being no more. This is their law. (*Confessions* 4.10)

The "law" of which St. Augustine speaks places the philosopher before the mystery of being and nothingness.

20

Death Reveals Being-with-Nothingness

I know now that I possess nothing, not even the beautiful gold of these decaying leaves, and still less these days flying from yesterday unto tomorrow.
—Philippe Jacottet

"THEY HASTEN TO BE no more," says St. Augustine. Because things die, nothingness enters our consideration of being. First of all, death reveals the temporal structure of being, and thereby its radical contingency.

The philosopher is not the only one to experience this "contingence." C.-F. Ramuz, the poet, confides to us that the question of death assailed him at the tender age at which, in his boarding school, his Latin class was translating Caesar. Relating this early experience, speaking of the child that he was then, he writes:

> One day, he saw that he had begun to be, and that he had not always been, and that the death that was before him was likewise behind him—that he had ceased for a moment to be dead to live, and that he would have to cease, at another moment, being alive in order to be dead. . . . In class, when he was translating Caesar, it suddenly occurred to him to wonder, "Where was I in Caesar's time? What was I in Caesar's time?"[45]

Death introduces the temporal, and eventually, nothingness, into the heart of being. Time evinces its nature as elusive, precisely because it is essentially related to nonbeing. Once again we must heed the words of St. Augustine. On the question of time, he applies his dazzling power of dialectic as follows. Considering that time occurs in the past, the present, and the future, he asks:

> How, then, can these two times be, the past and the future? But the past is no longer, and the future is not yet. With regard to the present, if it were always present, if it were not to join the past, it would not be time, it would be eternity. If the present, then, being time, must reunite with the past, how can we state that it also is, since it can only be by ceasing to be? Thus, what allows us to affirm that *time exists,* is that it *tends to exist no more.* (*Confessions* 11.15)

Applying these reflections, we must say, then: Yesterday this hyacinth was not at all—tomorrow it will not be at all. Being temporal, its being is an apparition between two nothingnesses!—the nothingness of before and the nothingness of after.

Up to this point, the existence of things in nature has appeared to us as an act whereby things hold fast with matter. Now, because of their "death before and after," their existence is revealed as surrounded by nothingness. Now the verb "to be" flashes forth in an absolutely new meaning. Suddenly it appears as the act that wrests things from nothingness and holds them above nothingness.

Until now, when we predicated being of things, we emphasized their base, the subject from which they emerge and in which they subsist. We witnessed the effort they expend on matter itself. Now, thinking of the time when they were not at all, and the time when they will no longer be at all, we see opening up a kind of abyss. Beneath them, there is nothing. There is nothingness!

And so the philosopher is astonished to see that the same word, "to be," the same verb, actually has two meanings, with analogies between them, but only analogies. What a difference between the act of thrusting forth from matter and subsisting at the heart of matter, and the act of standing fast above nothingness! This act defines metaphysical being, because it can no longer be contemplated in relation to a preexisting matter but must be contemplated in relation to nothingness.

Looking back to the earlier chapters of this book, we could indicate this double meaning of the verb "to be" in the following manner.

Until now we have contemplated, in things, their "to be substance." We have considered things as supported by a matter worked and built up by a form. Now, the act of being that we are about to contemplate could be called "existence being." We mean by this word "existence"—according to its etymology, "standing out"—"a pure activity, a consistence, but superior to the entire order of the imaginable."[46]

In the second part of this book, we are going to attempt to say something about this new depth of "being." It is to another mystery of being that we seek to turn our regard. From now on, the object to be pursued will be existence, the act of existence—which we shall call, with Maritain, a "victorious thrust" by which all things "triumph over nonbeing."[47]

Part 2

There is no philosophy so profound and so subtle that it cannot be, and ought not to be, expressed in everyday language.

—Henri Bergson

Introduction

BERGSON'S IDEAL was to transmit philosophy in everyday language. And he did not allow this desire to remain purely theoretical. His work is presented in an elegant, clear language—free of all technical heaviness. In the art of being simple in philosophy, he was a real expert!

Bergson's reflection, used as the epigraph of our second part, encourages us in our intent: to transmit a philosophy of being with as little recourse as possible to a specialized vocabulary.

In our first part, this was relatively easy to do. We had to describe the "act" of the being of nature while remaining in contact with sensible experience: a seed that sprouts, a flower opening out to the sun. But now, in approaching the properly metaphysical domain, the "act" of being that we are about to contemplate is different. It consists in wresting things from nothingness, holding them above nothingness. Clearly, we can no longer, we ought no longer, describe it as before. In particular, the intelligence will no longer rest on sensible reality alone.

The very word "metaphysics"—does one not spontaneously think of an obscure, esoteric knowledge? And yet we think it possible, even in a knowledge that "the gods envy us," to speak simply. Bergson encourages us to persevere.

21

On Existence

Have you never raised your mind to an under-standing of existence in and for itself–in the sole fact of existing? . . . Had you truly been able to manage this, you would have felt the presence of a mystery, which would have pierced your soul with wonder and fright.

—Samuel Taylor Coleridge

NOW WE MUST "think existence" in and for itself. We shall attain this if we see that the energy exercised, exerted, by existence is of another order from the energy exercised by corporeal substance in thrusting itself to the light. The realization of a form from matter is surely not the same thing as to realize something from nothing. Existence gives a being to hold up above nothingness. As we see, the verb "to be" is freighted with another meaning.

To grasp what the term "exist" means is to sense that it expresses a great mystery. Indeed, it expresses the presence and activity of an energy that communicates to a being to emerge from the abyss of nothing. The mystery resides in the fact that this extreme energy exerted by the "existing" thing is not possessed by the thing in itself. It is not its cause. However profoundly the mind descends into its structural elements,

77

existence is not there. In fact, if existence were a constitutive part of the things of this world, they would not have to appear one day and disappear on another day. Existence, then, is not in the power of the things that it activates. It is precisely because of this that, when existence causes a thing to "appear," it plunges the mind in mystery. In addition, the one who awakens to existence is astonished at not having been astonished before. And Romanian playwright Eugène Ionesco asks, "How has the world, how has existence, managed to appear to me, usually, as 'natural,' as 'normal'? Only in routine is everything normal. Existence, creation, cannot be normal."[1]

To raise the mind so as to see existence necessarily means entering into mystery. We have observed above that a species does not actually exist. Only individuals exist. Existence is attributed to that which, in the order of things, is individual, unique: to this rose, this swallow. But this rose, this swallow, *did not exist* yesterday, and tomorrow they will *no longer exist.* Thus, the individual advances toward us as an "apparition" between two nothingnesses! The consideration of the individual as such—the consideration of what is unique in a thing— also gives rise to a sensation of strangeness.

"The pure joy of existing sets me a-tremble."[2] This impression of a miracle is understandable. The keen perception of the individual is most often accompanied by an intuition that is not formulated. But we could formulate it in this way: It is not the species that in this thing is the cause of the individual. Of itself, the species, concerned as it is to maintain itself, remains indifferent to the individual. Rather, the species demands that the individual sacrifice itself for the sake of the species. No, the power, the energy that withdraws an individual thing from the abyss does not come from the species. This power, this energy of existence can only be the effect of a cause for which the unique individual has a value. Existence can be produced only by the being that is pure act. It requires a pure energy, capable of overcoming the abyss of nonbeing and attaching itself to this individual thing precisely because it is individual and unique.

> O my God, now I know that each thing
> contains its own mystery, and that you know the mystery.[3]

When the intelligence is visited with such intuitions, existence ceases to be a simple fact. True, most of the time it is not perceived for itself. Everyone sees it, but without seeing it! To appreciate it in its own mystery is something like a grace. Maritain once acknowledged that it had in it something "evangelical." He said of being as existence: "Like the numerous poor, it lies hidden in the light. There, I believe, is a characteristic, a general property, of the highest things." And seeking to clarify its mystery, but without using a philosophical vocabulary, he adds: "What I then perceive is something like a pure energy, a consistency, but superior to any imaginable order—a vibrant tenacity by which things burst forth at me, surviving any possible disaster."[4] It also occurs that the awareness of existence in and for itself prompts in the soul another affective tonality. Coleridge cites the emotion of "fright." The vision of the "appearance" of something caught between two "nothingnesses" reveals the abyss just beneath itself. Ionesco wonders: "What is the enigma *under* this appearance, *under* this mask of serenity? Yes. The enigma is there, always. The problem: What is there *behind* and *under* the finery? Incredible existence, source of wonderment!"[5]

To see what is individual and unique in things, existence, means sounding the remotest depths of being. Yet this fierce energy which sustains being could also assume the aspect of a blind, dreadful, and obscure power before the enormous spectacle inherent in the mass of things that exist. But this feeling becomes neutralized when we also recognize that the individual is sustained in time in order to accomplish a program, and

to realize an *idea,* in order to play its "role" with a view to the
common good. With regard to the program things have to
accomplish, to the "idea" they must realize, and to the "role"
they must maintain, philosophers also give a name. They call
them: their "essence."

22

On Essence 1

Water knows water; mind scents essence.
                              —Paul Claudel

T HE CONTEMPLATION of existence, of that victorious
power over nonbeing, frequently awakens the mind of the
philosopher to the numberless variety of forms existing
beyond the abyss. In nature, existence never occurs by itself.
To be sure, it is the basic act, but always the act of something
altogether determinate: this tulip, this titmouse, this star. It is
a matter of an immediate datum of the mind. One does not
have to prove the unimaginable multiplicity of the forms of
being; one has only to open one's eyes.

True, for the most part, we are scarcely surprised at existence, and still less at what it sustains above nothingness. The
genius of metaphysics will always be to marvel that the act of
existence, with its own energy, is always at the service of something. "Something": yes, here we have another familiar word to
which the philosopher will attach a special meaning. To the
philosopher, this word means that the power of existence is
entirely applied to keep from the abyss an altogether determi-

nate entity—in other words, an entity specifically determined to accomplish its task, to play its part, and to achieve its purpose. As Claudel exclaims, "Oh, the forces at work around me!"[6]

These determinate things, which make their way toward their end in order to be fulfilled, are called, in philosophy, "essences." Let us pause over this word. It comes from the Latin infinitive *esse,* which is translated "to exist." Phonetically, it is clear that the word "essence" is immediately related to the verb *esse.* The term "essence," then, indicates in things their first determination, specifying that this determination finds in existence its very first connection.

In part 1 of this book, we called "substantial form" what makes a rose a rose and not a tulip, a titmouse a titmouse and not a swallow. Then we considered the being of the thing in its work of self-construction and in its effort to *maintain* what it has made itself. Now we are calling this same substantial form an "essence," because we are viewing it under the precise angle of its relation to existence—of its relation precisely to the act that *sustains* it over the abyss of nonbeing.

In order to place this relationship in a clearer light, we must consider how things "hold on" to their existence. To reach this end, we must make ourselves sensitive to the constant care, the stubborn application, that plants and animals, for example, maintain in order to accomplish the program that they have before them. We find an example of this determination in the work of the fig tree, which Rilke watched with such passionate intensity. He said that he was particularly struck to see it preoccupied above all to form its fruit, without lingering over "the glory of the flowers." Addressing this tree as if it were a person, he says:

> Fig tree, for a long time this has been a sign to me,
> that you almost entirely bypass blossoms

and press your pure secret,
without ostentation, in the early-chosen fruit.
Like the pipe of a fountain
your bent branches propel the sap
downwards and up again:
and it springs forth from sleep,
almost without awakening,
in the happiness of its sweetest achievement.[7]

The poet could have directed this same attention to any plant, any animal.

We should see, then, that everything here below goes its vigorous way toward its fulfillment, its most precious good. Whoever has the leisure to contemplate in things the joy they take in working by way of their being, understands what "essence" means. It not only means a capacity to exist, but still more, inscribed in their very roots, it includes the profound desire to keep for themselves an existence miraculously received!

23

On Essence 2

What could be more mortal for a perishable being
than to exhale the eternal, and for a second inexhaustible,
fragrance of a rose?
The more something dies,
the more it arrives at its internal end–
and the more it expires
in this word that it cannot say
and this secret that draws it!

—Paul Claudel

WE SHOULD LIKE TO TAKE yet another route to a vision of what essence contributes to existence. To this purpose, we listen to a philosopher who has removed essences from any consideration of the act of being. This is how Jean-Paul Sartre sees things: "This plane tree with its bark cover, this oak half-decayed, some would have me take them for young, keen energies flinging upward toward the sky!" The roots of a chestnut tree have on him the effect "of a black and gnarled lump, altogether ugly," or "a long, dead serpent at my feet." As he glances about, distorting what he sees, he seeks to take account of these beings by emphasizing only their decrepitude. Then, enunciating what he takes for a universal law, he concludes: "Things—we would have called them thoughts—they cease en route, have forgotten themselves, have forgotten what they wanted to think, and have remained in this condition, swaying about in a joke that makes little sense."[8]

Sartre, we see, begins by emptying things of their dynamic,

of the surge that carries them to their purposes. He has no use for their youthful energies. He blinds himself to the happy thrust that leads them to their flowers and their fruits. But this radical evacuation of essences leads him fatally to underestimate existence: "These trees—they had no desire to exist; they simply could not prevent it. There you have it. Yes, they did all their little recipes quietly, without zest. The sap runs slowly in their ducts, and reluctantly."[9] In Sartre's kitchen, unlike that of Heraclitus, we never meet the gods!

One day, however, he raised an objection to his own doctrine. "Evidently, I did not know everything [about the chestnut tree]. I had not seen the seed developing, nor the tree growing."[10] But he immediately turns aside from the task of describing the thrust of the seed, the stages of its growth, its flowers and fruits. Why this reluctance?

Sartre does violence to things, bracketing their origin and growth, their fruitfulness. The result could only be a defective vision. After an exercise like the one he maintains, being emerges as bloodless, flat, sick, "nauseous"! After having "denatured" and "de-essenced" things, Sartre attempts to show that it is existence's turn to be smitten with absurdity: "Every existent is born without reason. It continues by weakness, and dies by chance."[11]

Had he been willing to contemplate the young plane tree, working mightily to make itself to be, Sartre would have been able to, would have had to, see how many things are attached to their existence precisely because they seek to achieve their purpose. Because the things of this world seek to state their whole meaning, to the extent that they do, they hold fast to their own existence. They want to exist. Because of their close connection to *esse* (the Latin verb that means "to exist"), we call them "essences." To one who appreciates this viewpoint, things are like thoughts, which exhaust what they are respon-

sible for saying, investing their being with the sweetness of
intelligibility.

To help us gain such a vision of being, poets and painters
are necessary and irreplaceable. Their charism enables this
intelligibility to radiate in things. They do so differently from
the philosopher and the scientist. It is by omitting the verb,
and an object's characteristics, that they unveil the essence
deep within objects. Picasso once said as much. "I have never
placed myself outside reality. I have always been at the very
essence of reality."[12] Is it not a vision of essence that Giacometti's *Cat* presents? (Remember, this is the same Giacometti who sculpts the void.) Removing more and more
matter, he is left with a transverse rod with a lump of metal at
the end, and four more rods, like two triangles, which move.
The Platonic essence of "cat" has just made its appearance.

Writers, too, succeed remarkably in evoking essence by calling on certain characteristics. One of them, for example, dis-
closes to us the intimate nature of a fox: "This smooth beast
with a gullet full of needles . . . those yellow eyes, almond
shaped, and the laugh shuddering in the muzzle; this lissome
lord hastening to his bloody vespers in the shade."[13]

Whether it belong to the poet, the philosopher, or the
painter, the vision of essences is a grace. This grace means
looking at things no longer as objects of use and consumption,
but as objects for contemplation. It is a grace to let them be
what they are. It is a grace to assist them to realize their eager
victory in reaching their desired purpose.

Why must we always regard things in connection with ourselves? Or, an arrogance still worse: Why must we believe that
we create these beings simply because we look at them? Leave
them to their own glory and to their own joy!

Granted, for such a grace we must pay its ransom. One day,
death and the decay of lovely things will cover each and every
one of them with a black veil. Operative, successful, and pow-

erful today, tomorrow they will grow weak, lifeless—finished. So attached to their existence—to the act that holds them beyond nothingness—they are nevertheless utterly incapable of preserving it. For any accurate celebration of being, there is always a major and a minor key—successively, yes, but inseparably. At times, even simultaneously!

> Atop the larch,
> still pink with winter and with frost,
> the first little bird perches,
> and whistles a long, bittersweet song—
> melancholy prelude to wild hymns.
> I know your pain, but then,
> whence comes your joy, O Life?[14]

24

The Music of Being

I *have at my disposition the seven notes of the scale,*
with its chromatic intervals. I have loud and soft.
And thus I have the solid, concrete elements that offer
me a field of infinite experience.

—Igor Stravinsky

THAT ONE IS A METAPHYSICIAN for whom existence is
no longer a banality. One becomes a metaphysician the
day existence appears as the absolutely first act of all things.
This is the act that keeps them beyond nonbeing. Now they
exist above the abyss, and for this reason we call these things
"essences."

But intelligence does not awaken to this mystery without
also being awakened to the limitless variety of essences—of the
forms of being. As Stravinsky says: ". . . a field of infinite experience." For a moment, then, let us think of the different kinds
of the real: mineral, vegetable, animal. Let us think also of
species, and their innumerable subspecies. And what shall we
say when we recognize the even broader limitlessness of individuals! We are led to compare being to a musical theme, inexhaustible in its keys and its rhythms. Still, no musical universe
can rival the fertility of being's theme.

We have to say: The theme of being is made up of only two notes, essence and existence. But in the realm of being, two notes make a chord! Of itself, this rapport excludes no possibility. Always, whatever form it takes, being is something determinate, which maintains itself outside nothingness (existence). But this rapport, because it contains only two terms, is indefinitely variable.

It has been remarked that Mozart's genius consists in elaborating a theme from an extraordinary simplicity, two or three notes at times, into an immense architectural sonority. Mozart's melody can be a tiny seed, but it is a seed capable of growing into an immense, harmonious tree. This is the case with being. The motif of the most hidden being is pregnant with more variations than all the symphonies in the world.

The metaphysician becomes aware not only of the multiplicity and variety of the forms of being, but of their hierarchy as well. With the real, the metaphysician is given, in a flash of light, to see that being involves modes of value organized among themselves according to "more" and "less." There is the hard texture of the rock; we find more being, however, in the "living silk" of the peony and the rose. There is still more being in the "stretch" of the bird's desire. And what can we say of the agility of the human mind, quicker than lightning, which moves, without hindrance, in space and time?

Finally, let us hear Jacques Maritain, a great metaphysician, who conveys to us his vision of the manifold quality of things as follows:

> I see [being] as an intelligible reality bursting forth in the least thing, and valid for all things, but in different ways. It is as if one severed a blade of grass and there emerged something greater than the world—something that, with values and meanings essentially varied, reveals the cause of myself and of all that is.[15]

Being, then, offers to the metaphysician's mind two elements—"the most solid and concrete" elements, essence and existence. It is not for metaphysicians to determine the number and variety of their realizations. They are present before them. They encounter them and discover them. The limitless field of being is already open for them, inviting them to an infinite mystery!

25

Analogy of Poets

*I bring to everything its deliverance. Through me,
nothing is any longer alone. In my heart I associate
it with something else.*

— Paul Claudel

I T I S N O T A L W A Y S A W O N D E R I N G astonishment that is
promoted by the burgeoning of being's theme. In certain
minds, the enormous quantity of things, having no apparent
order, causes anxiety. What does this mass of beings of all
kinds, snatched from nothingness, jostling one another in the
realm of chance, mean?

But this sensation of strangeness and alienation disappears
the moment that—even for a second—under this tangled variety
of things, a certain unity nevertheless makes its appearance.
When an affinity of things, remote or proximate, is discerned,
the "nausea" vanishes. Things are rescued from the absurd.

The poet's mission, in particular, effects this salvation. "I
bring to everything its deliverance," says Claudel.[16] Thanks to
the poets, nothing remains alone. Poets reveal to each thing
that it is not a waste, since another thing, somewhere in the
world, needs it!

But what is a poet? Let us listen further to Claudel as he celebrates his own vocation. In his eyes, that vocation is greater than that of Caesar or Columbus: "My wish is to be the gatherer of God's earth."[17] Out of this mass of so many, various, even contrary things, he seeks to create a unity. The poet is charged with a peaceful mission. For his part, Pierre Reverdy gives his own definition: "The poet is an oven for roasting the real."[18] He means that poets' inner flame fuses, in their incandescent heart, the most disparate things.

With these definitions, we are far removed from the superficial notion of a poet as one who makes up rhymes, "a maker of gewgaws and music boxes."[19] On the contrary, the poet is driven by a duty to traverse the world in search of things—things at times quite removed from one another by space, time, and even their nature. The poet is responsible for calling them together, in order to reveal to them their mysterious kinship. Reverdy has written profoundly of this phenomenon. "External reality does not live in poetry as it does outside. It is transformed there, and occasions a bursting forth of relationships."[20] But it is precisely in their reciprocal relations that things find their salvation.

There is more. The poetic intelligence has the power to pierce the wall of the material world, as well. For the poet, according to Baudelaire, "everything is a hieroglyph."[21] The poet senses that the things of this world bear supernatural meanings. The poet understands their language—understands that they speak of something else, of the world of the soul and God. With the flower, the bird, the fig tree, the cloud, did Jesus not evoke the hidden mysteries of the reign of God?

Baudelaire also wished the work of the poets to be taken seriously. "With the finest poets," he said, "there is no metaphor, no simile, no epithet that is not mathematically exact."[22] He added that poetry, like any other science, has a precise sphere for its inventory. For Baudelaire, this sphere consisted in the "inexhaustible fund of universal analogy."[23]

Indeed, it is thanks to analogy that the poet has the power to gather up and hierarchize the real. The word "analogy" comes from the Greek adverb *ana,* meaning a movement from below to above; and from *logos,* which means "reason." Analogy is therefore the quality possessed by reason to be able to move throughout all the degrees of being. It elevates material things to spiritual things because of the resemblances perceived between them. And then it reunites them.

We must emphasize once more: Poets do not create these resemblances, these affinities. They discover them. Ramuz even remarked, "These relations are imposed,"[24] forced on the poet! The result of these discovered relationships is the universe of symbols.

The symbol is the poet's country—the representation proper to the poet's intelligence. "Symbol" also comes from the Greek—from *syn,* meaning "with," or "together," and *ballein,* which means "to throw." The symbol "throws together" in the mind two things, quite different in themselves, but mysteriously united. With Mallarmé, for example, the swan represents at the same time the bird, and the poet, by reason of resemblances that only the poet, in this case, knows and evokes. Paralyzed by the contempt of those around him, the poet resembles the swan imprisoned by ice. By the symbol, two or more things are gathered together. The poet celebrates their kinship, exorcising their solitude and thereby revealing their mysterious oneness.

Thanks to the "poetic" analogy, nature is no longer this dark, inescapable forest. It has become a "forest of symbols."[25] Under the revealing eye of the poet, things of nature, things of the soul, and things of God discover kinships that astonish, and often enchant, poets. The genius of the biblical psalmist joins what is most spiritual with what is most physical: "God is my rock!" (Psalm 18:2).

26

The Metaphysical Analogy 1

At the root of metaphysical knowledge, Saint Thomas places the intellectual intuition of that mysterious reality concealed beneath the most common and banal word in our language: the word "be."

—Jacques Maritain

T HE POETIC ANALOGY sets in relief a tendency consubstantial to the human intellect: to unite things even the most distant, even opposed. God and rock, spirit and water. To gather the world together is poets' passion. Their intuition communicates to them, again, the power of lifting themselves upward from the things of this world toward realities that transcend it:

> Happy the one who, on nimble wing,
> soars toward the luminous fields and serene.[26]

But the leap of the poet to the higher regions is accomplished indirectly. By this we mean that poets do not use words according to their direct sense. For example, they apply the word "rock" to God, or "water" to the Spirit. Poets know quite well that these images do not *directly* describe the nature of the things.

True, then, the poet cannot join God and rock by reason of

a common nature. How different the nature of a rock and that of God! Why does the poet bring them together? While they do not really share the same nature, still, rock and God have in common that each is a principle of strength and stability, each according to its own modality. We note that the basis for the poetic analogy is a resemblance, but a resemblance in aspects external to things: their actions, their behavior, their shapes.

The proof that reason rises "obliquely" in virtue of this "analogy" is that it subjects it to words that serve it as modifications.

Or else it is introduced by the adverb "as." Reason then wishes to transmit that it attains but an approximation:

> *As* long echos that, from afar, are confused
> into a murky, deep oneness,
> vast *as* night and *as* the brilliance of day.[27]

Or else the poet shows that words are used as metaphors. That is, the sense of the words is transferred beyond their proper area. "Metaphor" comes from the Greek *meta*, "beyond," and *pher-*, "carry." The metaphor is the privileged procedure of the poet. There is no longer any need to take the detour of a comparison. The rapprochement is effected immediately, like a bolt of lightning between two things. The poet's analogy is therefore called "metaphorical analogy."

> The lion's ferocious chrysanthemum head.[28]

After these last observations, we can speak of the metaphysician's analogy. It too has the power to unify things. It too communicates to the mind a way of soaring, by the ladder of things, all the way to God. But these two functions are exercised by the metaphysician in an entirely different way from the poet's fashion.

First, the metaphysician discovers that all entities, without exception, are interrelated. The metaphysician gathers them all under the same name, "being." All things, indeed, have that in common: being. Being means exercising the act of existence, the same act, whereby they are plucked from nothingness. By reason of existence, all of them triumph over the abyss. To be sure, among them the distance can be great, even infinite. At first glance, for example, what connection can there be between God and a blade of grass? Nevertheless, both of them are constituted by the same relation to existence. By reason of this relation, the intellect reconciles both of them. All things, then, share in existence, no matter what their species may be. And so it is the relation that each one maintains with existence that grounds all things in the metaphysical resemblance.

Moreover, the word "being" as applied to material as well as to spiritual things is never a metaphor. When one predicates the term "being" of God and then of a blade of grass, its meaning has not changed. Always and every time it indicates in these realities (and in all others) what is most basic: an essence and an existence and their connection. And we admit that this bipolarity of essence and existence occurs according to proportions infinitely diverse and variable. That is why we call this analogy the "analogy of proportionality."

The metaphysical analogy finds its source within each being. That is why reason covers all the categories of the real. In fact, it rises from a blade of grass to God, thanks to the infinite facility of the idea of being and the term that signifies it. Reason does not need to adjust the word "being" to any transfer of meaning.

In the word "being," the most simple and the most ordinary in our language, is something of the infinite, if almost always hidden. Martin Heidegger (1889–1976) has observed that "current language is nothing more than a forgotten poem, exhausted by usage, whose call has all but died away."[29]

The point is to rescue, from the wear and tear on the word "being," its original sense. This word keeps its power of making the intellect rise all the way to God, certainly, easily, truthfully. What grace attaches to this word when its first destination is known! We gather that destination having discovered this original sense. We understand that, having discovered this sense, Heidegger would describe the paradoxical destiny of being in the form of this litany:

> Being is what is most common to all,
> and at the same time uniqueness itself.
> Being is what is most taken for granted,
> and at the same time it is the starting point of all.
> Being is the surest support,
> while being also the a-byss [Ab-Grund].[30]

But fundamentally, is it not from the idea of being that abides in the spiritual unconscious of every person, that religious intuitions occur—the sense of the sacred, so evident throughout the history of religions in humanity?

27

The Metaphysical Analogy 2

*If the sense of being
and the love of being,
were pure and absolute,
then we would see the world suddenly re-emerge
in an extraordinary splendor, in Edenic nakedness—
a rose all new and transparent,
made of relations with God.*

—Dom Vermeil

THE WORD "BEING," if uttered in the fire of a true intuition, is endowed with the miraculous power to "gather" all things together in unity. In spite of their wide differences of genus, species, and individual, the verb "to be" declares their affinity. Indeed, all things resemble one another in the relation of their essence to their existence.

Again, the word "being" reveals to them their affinity because they belong to a common cause, a single source. Let us see why.

In the region in which we live, the being we encounter is always a limited being. Yesterday it was not. Tomorrow it will no longer be. This tree: it is from being that it has begun. Being does not belong to it. Like everything else that is born and dies, it contains only one part of being. In this region where we are, we actually find only participated being, and therefore a received, caused being.

But if the being that we encounter is a participated being, then the being that causes all things ought to be called "being-in-itself," or "absolute being," the being we call God. St. Thomas says, "God, whom we cannot name except by working from the divine effects, is named 'Being' altogether accurately" (*On the Divine Names* 5.2).

The beings I encounter here below, then, are the effects of God. All things, if I consider them from the viewpoint of a received and participated act of existence, depend on God. Despite their differences, all of them are joined in the same community of dependency. All are suspended from, as it were, attached to, the same unique being that causes them. Among themselves they maintain a "community of belonging to God," who is the source of all being in things.

Having followed the path of things that lead the intellect to God, let us take the reverse route. We can say: Since all things depend on Being-in-itself, since it is from it that they receive their existence, then they have a right to be denominated being. St. Thomas observes: "It is relative to existence itself that God is participated first of all and before every other perfection" (*On the Divine Names*, no. 633).

The analogy that binds all things to God because they depend on God, receives the name, "analogy of attribution." The noun "being" passes from things to God and from God to things, uniting all to God and God to all. This analogy, based on a total dependence by participation, grounds the connection between creature and Creator.

St. Augustine was profoundly affected by this analogy. His genius has dramatized its mystery. The relationship of all beings in their common dependence upon the God of all things is expressed by these beings, he says, in a cry: "They cry out because they have been created, for they change and vary. . . . They cry out also because they have not created themselves: 'We are because *all* of us have been created. Therefore we were not before being. We cannot create ourselves'" (*Confessions* 11.4).

By reason of the things that it first meets, the intellect sees being as presenting this first cleavage. Being is distinguished between the being that is caused and the being that causes, between participated being and the being that causes participation. Thus there arises the twin relationship of the creature to the Creator, between the being that confers being and the being that receives it. Then indeed, as the contemplative has observed, the world arises before the gaze as "the universal Rose made from its relations to God."

St. Augustine prays: "It is you, then, who have created them—you who are beautiful for they are beautiful, you who are good for they are good, you who *are* for they *are*. But they are not perfectly beautiful, or good, or existing, as are you, their Creator" (*Confessions* 11.4).

28

The Transcendentals: Ladder of Being

All of the great words are synonymns, or tend to become such. . . . Order, oneness, truth, beauty, goodness. . . . They are constructed in a pyramid: that is, they desire to merge, and suppose a meeting point, as if we had no religion and they had one.
—Charles-Ferdinand Ramuz

THE THREE PRECEDING CHAPTERS have taught us of the marvelous power of words. Words not only serve us in matters of utility: they also have the vocation to signify the extraordinary kinship of things, of all things among themselves. It is quite true that intellect charges them with this mission. It obliges them to infinite versatility. If words are physical movers, intellect gives them, as it were, their soul.

First we saw this with the poets. The "wonderful relationships" of things among themselves intoxicates the poets. In order to articulate their unexpected affinities with others, the poets effect relationships on the words themselves, by simile or by metaphor:

> Like a lion, he has broken all my bones. (Isaiah 38:13)

> O shepherd Eiffel Tower! How the flock of bridges bleats this morning![31]

101

Next, we observed the same phenomenon with the metaphysician. There are still other relationships, more intimate ones, which metaphysicians discern among things. To indicate these, they have recourse to analogous terms. These, such as "being," do not have to surrender their primary sense. One and the same word, like "being," indicates things altogether distant and removed from one another. Still, it is correct to predicate "being" of God and of a blade of grass. Indeed, each is constituted intrinsically by the relation that obtains between its essence and its existence. We have already established this—being bears within itself this relationship: something that exists.

Finally, the word "being." The metaphysician employs it to signify still another rapport among things: the relationship of a *common dependency*. When the same perfection is predicated of two things of which one is the cause and the other the effect, they have the right to bear the same name. Thus, a climate is called "healthy," and even more the organism is "healthy" in which the climate causes health. The metaphysician who sees that being is caused, participated in, in the things of this world, is required to go right to the top, that is, to the first cause, to being in itself, which alone causes being. Ramuz expresses it felicitously: such a word is "constructed in a pyramid."

But there are other words as vast as being. Among these "great words" the metaphysician cites four: oneness, truth, beauty, and goodness.

Instead of saying, poetically, that these words are "constructed in a pyramid," the philosopher calls them the "transcendentals." "Transcendental" comes from the Latin *trans,* meaning "across," and *ascend-,* "to rise," "to make an ascent." These four words—"oneness," "truth," "beauty," and "goodness"—have the same power, then, as "being." They span all of the categories of the real, without having to alter their first meaning. They are attributed to all things, for what they express suits all things without exception.

St. Thomas Aquinas says of oneness, truth, goodness, and beauty that they are "the inseparables" from "being" (see *Scriptum super libros sententiarum* d. 8, q. 1, a. 3). The objects denoted by these words are as "great" as that denoted by being, since they circulate everywhere on the ladder of things. And St. Thomas adds: "Never do they abandon one another": *Numquam derelinquunt se.*

Other words are attributed only to limited categories. "Oak," for example, is limited in itself, limited to its vegetable kind and to the species of tree that it denotes. The word "titmouse" belongs to the animal kingdom, and to one species alone. If these words are attributed to something else, they are withdrawn from their proper domain.

The transcendentals, on the contrary, relate to all kinds of things, to all species of plant and animal, for example, and this without bursting forth from, changing, their first meaning.

As we see, the transcendentals enjoy a wondrous naming capacity. Their power comes from the fact that the intellect has seen that the perfections signified by oneness, truth, goodness, and beauty are found—like that of being, indeed—interior and intimate to all things without exception.

How could we fail to revere, in some sort, these words, which guide and bear us from this world to the domains in which being is divested of matter—to the domain of feelings, to that of the intellect, to the moral domain, to God! Ramuz acknowledges the merit of these words when he says in their regard: "It is as if, ourselves having no religion, they had one, and of themselves, outside us, tended to unity."[32]

29

Oneness, or Consistence of Being

*Things are really, evidently offered to our knowledge.
They are hierarchized, and present a mysterious
oneness, whose quest is the passion of the mind. They
steer us toward God, and thereby merit our gratitude.*
—Dom Vermeil

WE NOW PROPOSE to pursue each of the transcendentals in order—each of the perfections that accompanies being, all being. In each of these transcendental perfections, one of the traits of being as such will appear. When our task is complete, what a lavish, splendid tableau we shall behold!

In order really to grasp these inseparable perfections of being, which "do not leave it ever," we must contemplate them precisely in the act exercised by being. We must always revive the intuition that renders the intellect sensitive to being.

And first, let us consider material being, at the moment it makes its first approach to the light. For example, let us think of a seed that thrusts its way through its shell and "invents" a tree. See, it emerges from itself: roots, trunk, branches, leaves. The multiple organs of which the tree has need, it powerfully attaches to. It joins them to itself so intimately that a branch cut away, a leaf plucked, dies. Branches, leaves, indeed all of the other parts that make up the tree have being only in and by the aggregate, only in and for the whole. We have shown in part 1 that the being of a body is the energy with which it constructs itself. But this energy is exerted precisely in the formation of its parts and their unification in a whole.

There is no separation possible between being and oneness. Being and oneness maintain an inseparable common thrust, and they die together if divided. Could there be any clearer proof that being is one? An observation of St. Thomas will offer a compendium of what we are saying. "What is multiple is not in possession of its being as long as its parts are divided, but only when they constitute and form the composition itself" (*STh* I, q. 11, a. 1).

This dictum is altogether applicable, as well, to being in its metaphysical sense. If we regard being as the act that maintains the essence of a thing above nothingness, we see that these first two components of being are also undivided. We have shown how essence, in all that exists, thrusts indefatigably toward its own operation:

> . . . As a little seed, too small to be identified,
> Cast upon good soil, whence it gathers
> all of its energies, and produces a specific plant.[33]

Yes, it is for this that the seed desires to live. Only through existence will it be able to realize its purpose so naturally desired. How would these two elements, the most basic in being, fail to unite themselves to one another? Once united, would they not try to maintain their unity? Existence confers on essence the power to realize the need it has of its purpose. ". . . as the tree, each year at the beginning of spring, animated by its soul, invents itself."[34]

For its part, essence bestows on existence, on this force that causes it to emerge from nothingness, its reason for being, its justification before mind. Yes, in the first instance, being represents the unity of an essence with its existence. Once again, St. Thomas teaches: "Being and one imply each other. Any being whatever *consists* in its indivisibility: from this comes the fact that, just as everything protects its own being, so also it protects its own oneness" (*STh* I, q. 11, a. 1).

In this way, then, oneness will be the first of the traits presented by the face of each being. It is its primordial consistency! To say, "Being is one," is equivalent to saying that being is an energy that welds and cements all of the parts of a thing into a single whole. Energy and inner cohesion imply each other. Internal division signs the death of the being.

Oneness, then, like being, is a transcendental perfection. It varies to an infinite degree. In the atom, the molecule, the cell, the bodily organism, in the mind, in God, oneness maintains itself with urgency. With each rung of the ladder of being, unity is reinforced. With corporeal beings, the higher we climb, the more numerous are the elements composing them—let us think, for example, of the millions of neurons in the brain of a human being—and the stronger must the oneness be that holds them together. In the domain of spirit, essence can no longer die, since there is no matter. What, then, is to be said when we arrive at the being whose essence is to exist? Here oneness attains simplicity.

In our presentation on the analogy of attribution, we have explained that God, because God is *Being* in sovereign fashion, is the cause of all participated being. Now we must also say: Since God is *One*, sovereignly, God is therefore the cause of all participated oneness in things.

We become sensitive to the ascent of oneness in the heart of things when we see it mount all of the rungs in the scale of being. We go from the oneness that manifests itself in the composition of bodies, to the more profound oneness of essence and existence. Then from there we go on to contemplate the divine oneness, where there is no composition. We realize, precisely in our contemplation of the divine oneness, that the unity contemplated in things is like the shadow of the divine unity cast upon them!

30

Truth, or the Light of Being

*Nothing is more intelligible for us than the fact that
we are knowing–cognizant, that is, of an ontological
wealth such that we live at one and the same time
our act, and that of a limitless quantity of objects: we
actualize ourselves in receiving the objective reality
of an indefinite quantity of foreign acts.*
                                                          —Dom Vermeil

I NOTICE THAT THE WORD "true" possesses a power identical to that of "being" and "one." I can attribute it to all
things and to each thing. No category of being has a monop-
oly on it. I can say, for example, "Here is a true diamond." But
I can also say, "Here is a true rose." Or again, "a true lion." I
can even make a judgment that will be expressed in the asser-
tion, "That is a true lie!" Finally, one addresses the "true God."
The word "true" is certainly a transcendental. It too runs
through the entire ladder of being.

What does this word mean? With the Greek philosophers,
what we call "true", they name *alēthēs*, which, when translated
etymologically, means "not veiled," "not forgotten." For the
ancient Greeks, Lethe was the river of forgetfulness.

To say of a thing that it is "true," then, is to say that it is
unveiled, revealed, that it gives itself to be known. To say of a
thing that it is "true" is to set it in relation with cognition.

Since the word "true" is a transcendental, since it is inseparable from being, we must ask what it is, in the human being, that is capable of knowing the being of things. The being of things is what is most profound in them—what most basically constitutes them, that is, their essence and their existence. Now, among the faculties of cognition in the human being, there is one that is ordered to know what in things is the most interior. It is called the "intellect." The word "intellect" comes from *intus,* which means "within," and *leg-,* meaning "read" (as well as "gather"!). It is the human being, then, and the human being alone, who, in this world, can read the interior of things. The human being is the only one to whom being gives itself to be known—and the only one, then, for whom being is "true," that is, unveiled, revealed.

But how is the being of things unveiled? To answer this, we must ask of things the following question: What is it? A child may ask this question as well as an adult. But if we look at it carefully, in this question the intellect inquires into both essence and existence. The former aspect seeks to say *what something is.* It seeks to define the essence, which it enunciates when it defines the thing. Then there is a second operation, the judgment. In the judgment, the intellect decrees that the essence grasped within the mind also exists outside of the mind. It decrees that this essence is placed outside nonbeing, in reality.

We can give an example. If someone asks, "What is this?" and I reply, "This is an oak tree," I am indicating a tree outside myself—*this.* Next, I indicate the essence: *oak tree.* Moreover, I affirm that existence keeps this essence above the abyss by articulating the verb "to be" in the present tense: *is.* In the simplest of sentences, we find the whole of metaphysics!

The intellect, in these two operations, actualizes a perfect accord or agreement between the being of things and itself. St. Thomas has defined truth as the "conformity of the intellect and the thing" (*STh* I, q. 16, a. 2). Truth actualizes a correspondence between the intellect, which questions, and the being, which is questioned. Being is "true" when the intellect responds to it.

Two centuries before Aristotle, Parmenides (sixth century B.C.) had already proclaimed this accord. One can say that the birthday of metaphysics was the day Parmenides proclaimed the indissoluble relationship between being and thought. "The act of thought and the object of thought are intermingled. Without the being upon which it pronounces, you cannot know what the act of thinking is."[35]

Heidegger compares this sentence to a caryatid. Motionless and pure, she stands at the entrance of the Temple of Wisdom, like a statue before the Parthenon.

Yes, the intellect is the scion of being. It is for being. Its calling is to state being. In things, being is a font of light—but it is to intellect that it reveals itself as light. If no intellect existed, which would be impossible, being could say nothing at all. If existence had no essence above nothingness—as with Jean-Paul Sartre—intellect would not be able to say anything either. With the philosopher of the absurd, one should have to proclaim: "Being is eternally superfluous."

But this is not the way things are. The intellect questions and being responds. Being unveils to the intelligence what it is. On its face, then, appears this trait of light: truth.

But we must add at once: It is not the human being who creates essences. When the human being appeared on the scene of the world, things had already been thought. "There is a spiritual part even in raw bodies: it is the *form* that holds them in being."[36] Long before the human being appeared, the First Intelligence had set them above nothingness. A First Intelligence has thought and created the world in order for an intellect to understand them. Such is the duty of the human being!

The human being has been created first of all for this contemplation: "All of my joys have been in the relationship between myself, who am, not to what I have had, but to what is. The human being is born for contemplation. All of my happiness has come from that. . . . There is but one point to be attained, and it is but rarely attained—the act of adoration."[37]

31

The Good, or the Generosity of Being

Love concerns all that is–matter, heart, and spirit. It is interested not in the human being alone, but in the animal, and not only in the animal and the human being, but in the plant, and not only in the plant, but in the mineral–not only in the organic, then, but in the inorganic, as well, since love is concerned with all three realms. The word "love" must be used, because it, too, circulates from below on high, and from on high below, on the ladder of being.

—Charles-Ferdinand Ramuz

HERE IS A TEXT that, just by itself, would suffice to prove that metaphysics does not belong only to specialists. First of all we find this wonderful description of a transcendental: something and a word that "circulates from below on high, and from on high below, on the ladder of being." The vision of love as a transcendental perfection has come to Ramuz with the passionate and tender attention he brought to all things and to each one individually. His farewell to the things of this world indicates all the value that they have had for him. "I have too much loved the world," he says. "I see now that I have too much loved it. For the moment, then, it must evanesce."[38] Long has he regarded the love present in all things. The love by which everything present, the love which, like the angels of Jacob, descends and ascends the ladder of God!

To see love universally present means seeing the good

present everywhere. The good and love are correlative terms, for what is the good if not the being itself that is desired and loved? But all things are potential objects of a desire. Aristotle defined the good: "What all things—and each thing individually—desire" (*Ethics* 1.2; 1094a18).

Thus, stone is good for a statue. A seed is good for a bird. The horse for the farmer. Science for the human being. The list would be limitless! And what if we think that each thing loves its being as its nearest good! And that all beings love God more than themselves because they depend on God and receive from God that which basically constitutes them: essence and existence!

Here we must make an observation. If every being is good for another, it is because all of them communicate some perfection. To the need of one being, another responds, bestowing its good. The sun gives its warmth to the plant; water, its freshness to human beings. The flower, its fragrance; the bird, its song. The human being, his and her science and art. And God communicates being to all that is.

The good, then, is still another feature on the countenance of being. It is another "epiphany of being." It manifests its fundamental generosity. And this is its merit. A being loved, a being of which another being has need, deserves to be. In its capacity as true, being brings light; as good, it brings joy!

To be sure, there is a great deal of evil in the world—many absences, privations, lacks. But there are even more gifts, communications, "goodnesses." St. Augustine recalls that, in making the world, God experiences the joy of having made good things. He has counted them, and yes—seven times!

> You saw, O my God, all that you had created, and your works seemed excellent to you. For each kind of creature, after having said, "Let them be," and when they were, you saw that they were good. It is written seven times—I have counted them—and you saw the goodness of your work. And the eighth time, you contemplated your creation all together and you said that it was not only good, but excellent throughout. (*Confessions* 13.28)

32

Beauty, or the Splendor of Being

In order to encounter beauty and to secure it, one must renounce the realms and domains of the entire world, yes, and sea and sky. It is thanks to this renunciation and this disregard that one can turn toward it and contemplate it.

—Plotinus

B EAUTY, TOO, IS A PERFECTION that ascends and descends the ladder of beings. How often the word "beautiful" occurs in people's conversation! And apropos not only of works of art, but of all kinds of things. In his *Confessions,* St. Augustine declares his delight with the elements of nature. "We see the beauty of the waters, converging on the plains of the sea" (13.32).

Augustine even reproaches himself with loving too much the seductive light of the corporeal world: "the queen of colors, this light with which all that we see is flooded" (10.34). There are no bodily forms—minerals, vegetables, animals—that have not been glorified by painters and sculptors eager to disengage this spiritual part of matter that fascinates them. Picasso never stopped painting an owl. Even the toad, under his gaze, undergoes a metamorphosis and is recast in a new truth. The lines from the *Cherubic Wanderer* might fit here:

In God's brightness,
nothing is grotesque, nothing bizarre;
The frog is as perfect as the archangel.[39]

Transcendental beauty made its entrance into philosophy with Plato's *Symposium,* the "Banquet." Here Socrates (fifth century B.C.) recounts how he was initiated to the contemplation of the ocean of beauty. The Lady Diotime, prophetess of Mantinea, after a consideration of the beauty of bodies, conducted him into that province of beauty which is the beautiful sciences: the beauty of a mathematical demonstration; the beauty of geometrical forms; the beauty of logical constructions (see *Symposium* 210a–211c).

Then Diotime introduced Socrates into the domain of beautiful moral actions: the actions of the heroes and saints, where beauty flashes in a blaze even more exquisite. It is in human flesh, in the flesh of the human heart, that a spiritual force suspends persons above the weighty load of their nature. Plotinus (third century A.D.) passionately remarks: "Neither the morning star nor the evening star are as beautiful as the face of justice and temperance" (*Enneads* 1.6).

Beauty, then, is in everything everywhere.

But what is beauty? The reflection in which we have just been engaged reveals its universality, along with the various degrees of its perfection, which clearly shows that beauty, like the one, the true, and the good accompany being itself—that it is another of the traits of the face of being.

But how may we define it? St. Thomas Aquinas says of beauty that it is "that whose sight pleases" (*quae visa placet; STh* I, q. 5, a. 4, ad 1). Beauty, then, relates a thing to vision, and thereby too establishes a relationship to a person's profound affectivity. Beauty is a joy, a delight. One could say: "Beauty is the very being of a thing whose knowledge awakens an ecstatic love, a rapture."

But we must be careful. When St. Thomas says that beauty is associated with the sight, he does not mean that it is the senses that grasp it—that it is "sensible" in itself. He is seeking, in the manner in which the sense of sight knows, an intuitive knowledge of an analogy for saying how the intellect grasps beauty. Even if we ourselves most often grasp beauty in sensible things, nevertheless beauty is a spiritual light in the sensible. "That part of the spiritual that is in crude material things" already![40] But this beauty is received *intuitively* in the intellect, like color in the sight, in the very action of color upon the sight. There is "beauty," then, when the hidden being of a bodily or spiritual thing is present in an *immediate, intimate, penetrating* presence in the intellect itself.

This calls for explanation. When our intellect seeks to seize the essence of a thing, its profound being, generally speaking it arms itself with many ideas. It arranges them in propositions, and the propositions in reasonings. It procedes scientifically. Then it lays hold of the thing, of its nature, but it does so by way of a whole tool-kit of abstract representations. Thereby the thing is, as it were, held at a distance. It remains, so to speak, "before" the intellect. It is judged, weighed, catalogued.

But when, for one reason or another, a sympathy, an affinity, between this thing and ourselves arises—for example, a tree—then a "connaturality" arises between it and the knowing subject. The latter has become available, permeable, even vulnerable. To draw it closer, to suppress the distance, to bring the object into its interior, the intellect renounces concepts, reasonings, all these heavy means. It allows itself to enter into the translucid night, where there are no ideas, images, or judgments. Then the beloved, desired object can approach, can enter the mind, can spill within it its charge of light, without intermediaries. This possession of the thing by the intellect, procured by love in imposing upon that intellect the silence of concepts, overwhelms the spiritual will altogether, with the joy of finally having what it loves.

A poet has magnificently evoked this mysterious descent of things into the night of our subjectivity:

> I load up, in my night, like a vessel at a pier,
> Helter-skelter, passengers and sailors.
> And I extinguish the light in my eyes, in the cabins.
> I make friends with the great depths.[41]

33

Recapitulation

*Reproaches of a contemplative
to Jean-Paul Sartre:
He has never looked at a flower–
what can he know of the Universal Rose?*
                                        —Dom Vermeil

HAVING COME TO THIS POINT, let us recapitulate the chapters of this second part in order to show how the analyses made thus far are interconnected.

From the beginning of this book, we have asserted this very simple thing: the being of things, for one who is favored by the metaphysical intuition, is an *act*. It is not a state, nor a simple fact. In our first part, we have contemplated this act as it manages even matter in order to come to the light. "Being" means a force at work in matter as the sculptor's "idea" causes the desired shape and form to emerge from stone.

> Oh, but the rock is lovely!
> How faithful it is, how it guards the idea![42]

But this act—so mighty, so generous—is nevertheless not the reason for the existence of a thing. If the act by which a rose gives itself to be a rose were identical to the act by which it exists, then it would not have begun to give itself existence

merely yesterday, and it would not surrender existence tomorrow. By the manner in which it hastens toward its flowering, I
well see that, for it, it is good to exist! To exist, to emerge from
nothingness, to hold firm above nothingness, is an altogether
different act. The verb "to be" carries an ambiguity that must
be ceaselessly dispelled when we meditate on being.

In fact, the act by which a rose makes itself "be" a rose, or
by which a bird makes itself "be" a bird can be observed. Scientists describe their ontogenesis, marking the stages of the
process of being, from seed to death. The word "ontogenesis"
comes from the Greek *ont-*, which means "being," and *genesis,*
meaning the way in which something comes to be. The "genesis" of this being is available to experimentation.

But no one has ever been able to claim to have "seen" a
thing emerge from nothingness, to have assisted at an emergence from nothingness. There is no scientific instrument
whose object is nothingness! Only the intelligence can speak
of nothingness, since, as its name indicates—and we have
observed—only the intelligence descends to the hidden interior of things. Because this rose, yesterday, did not yet exist
and tomorrow it will exist no longer, the intelligence knows
that it appears between two nothingnesses, that it holds fast,
for a moment, above them. As for the senses, they do not see
nothingness. They do not see this rose *exist.* They only register
a presence—not the act of emerging from nothingness.

Existence, this miraculous force, draws a thing from nothingness only to envelop it in its act. It holds this rose, for a
moment, above nothingness in order to provide it with the
accomplishment of its own action, the one in which it finds its
good: to flower, to give its color-architecture to be contemplated. We rightly call a thing an "essence." For the first relationship, the most important one for them, is the one they
have to existence. But "to exist," in Latin, is *esse,* whence the
term "essence." When we call things "essences" we seek to

acknowledge in them their tendency to exist. These two halves of being—existence and essence, *esse* and *essentia*—are certainly made to be united.

In our fourth chapter, we observed that the universe in which we live offers the spectacle of a quasi-infinite multiplicity of essences. Whence the incredible variety of the theme of being: air, but stone; water, but fire; the oak, but the violet; the elephant, but the fly. Being can be preposterous, but infinitely serious, as well! Now, under these considerable differences, these essences are all akin in the relationship they maintain with the same existence, which they thereupon diversify according to their finality. It is there, on this foundation, that their resemblance lies, there that their kinship is founded—on this community of resemblance. Thus, the beings of our universe, while unlimited in number and variety, are not without bonds with one another, are not strangers to one another.

And there is more. Because these beings are born at a moment in time, and finish with time, existence is lent them. They have but a part of existence. Participating, then, merely in existence, they have all received it. They are all "attached" to one and the same Being, which communicates to them the part of existence that they maintain for a time. And so we have still another kinship among them—a kinship in this common dependency with regard to Being itself.

Then, in the intellect that discovers this mystery, a desire awakens: that of reaching Being itself, upon which this intellect knows that it depends—it along with all other beings. And since Being in itself, the Source of all existence, is called "God," the question therefore arises in this intellect how it can climb all the way to God. How is it possible to "say" God?

In chapters 8 through 11, we showed that being is a transcendental. Being traverses all categories. Along with oneness, truth, goodness, and beauty, being is one of the words "constructed in a pyramid," of which Ramuz speaks. Climbing from the mineral to the vegetable, from the vegetable to the animal, and from the animal to the human, there is nothing in them that would prevent their mounting still higher. Their versatility is limited to no area, no species. Thus, they can ascend to God.

The chapters devoted to the transcendentals—to these "great words constructed in a pyramid"—have demonstrated that the intellect—like Jacob's angels—can ascend the ladder of being. But how far? How can it ascend to the absolute Being?

We now propose to show that, for this ascent, the intelligence receives a hidden power, a seed of divine light, a premiere truth, a first principle. This power propels it toward God, as it were, in whom alone it sees that its demands for light find their resolution. This is what we should like to show in our concluding chapters.

34

Seeds of Divine Light

I sense the effort of the lawn,
Awake under so much snow,
And the effort of reason
In the spirit that protects it.
                    —Supervielle

THINGS HAVE THE POWER to lead us all the way to God.
This is their greatest merit. In our first part, because of
certain operations of the living being—its organization, its
development directed toward an end—we concluded to the
presence of an intelligence at work in these processes. Aristotle, the reader may remember, was struck with wonder
before the plan manifested by nature (see *On the Parts of
Animals* 1.5; 645a7–11). But the act of being, which we now
contemplate in its metaphysical aspect, goes further, opening
to us a path to God.

Here is why. Being—that is, the act by which things hold
themselves above nothingness—is not only the first principle
of things in their reality. It is also the principle of the knowledge of things in the intellect. It is the being within things that
the intellect primarily grasps in them. St. Thomas Aquinas
compares the first conception of the mind, and the first judgment that forms in the mind at the same time, to "seeds."

121

"What exist before any other representation in our intellect are 'seeds,' from which the whole of human knowledge will spring" (*De veritate*, q. 11, a. 1).

Be advised, however: It is not a matter of innate ideas for Thomas—of a set of a priori logical categories according to which things will have to be thought. Far from it. It is things themselves that, by themselves, deposit these "seeds" of light in our thinking. For Thomas, when we are born into the world, our intellect is without any form or any judgment. It is plunged naked into the ocean of things. But what it does carry within is a hunger for the intelligible element that fills corporeal beings with a spiritual light.

For example, let us take the trouble to analyze the question children ask before the world offered them by their senses. We shall then see that it is indeed the being of things for which our mind hungers. The child's everlastingly repeated question, "What is that?" contains, we see, the "to be," and at the same time inquires into the "whatness" of the thing that "be's"— *essence and existence,* the two elements that we have asserted at the beginning of our present part 2 to compose all being. Here, then, we have a striking, if everyday, example of the face that the human intellect is essentially ordered to the being of sensible things, as St. Thomas would have it. Here we have a veritable law of the mind, drawn from a grammatical analysis of a question everyone asks, and from infancy on!

The intellect never seeks to grasp anything but the being of things. And when it has seized this being, when it has answered its question—for example, by saying, "This is an oak"—at the same time and in the same act it implicitly specifies the first law of being. In this answer is included an "evidence"—an obvious fact—that this oak is absolutely opposed to being anything but itself, and is indeed far more opposed to not being anything at all. It is absolutely impossible that a being be at the same time itself and something else, and even more impossible that it be and not be at the same time. This first law, called the principle of contradiction, is inscribed in every being and therefore necessarily in each apprehension of the being of a thing by the intellect.

Once more let us state emphatically: This doctrine must not be interpreted as meaning that we came into the world with two pre-formed schemata: with innate ideas of being and of the principle of contradiction. On the contrary: it is in each act of thought that the intellect seizes both being and identity—existence and essence. Then, since the act of thinking is indefinitely repeated, these two primary data are like "seeds" in the mind. In them resides the origin of any further act of intellectual cognition.

More than being a font, a seed is also an evolutive force. The concept of being, and the principle of contradiction that always accompanies it, are endowed with an incredible power of light. First, they bear an evidence brighter than the sun does for the sense of sight. And like any seed, they concentrate within themselves an irrepressible demand for growth and expansion. These two lights—the concept of being and the first judgment, which accompanies it—implant in the mind an insatiable need to understand every being and everything in being!

When in the things of nature we examine, first, an acorn, and then an oak at the extremity of its height, breadth, and power, how astonished we are! Who would have thought that these two extremes could belong to the same being? We would never have imagined them to be united in the identity of one and the same being. The same must be said of the order of knowledge: we would never have been able to think that the idea of being and its first truth, which we draw at every moment from everything in nature, are organically and vitally linked to the idea of God.

It is the metaphysician's gift to feel, under this "snow of the mind," the "effort of reason" that grows to God.

35

An Immense Dynamism: At the Center of the Soul

More heavenly
than these twinkling stars
are the infinite eyes
that Night has opened in us.

—Novalis

"THE INTELLECT IS NO MORE conscious of being than is the body of the air it breathes."[43] It is the mark of a spirit intimately linked to a body to awaken to being in the night of the unconscious—to awaken to the immediate data of which we have spoken in the foregoing chapter. The concept of being and the judgment upon its necessary identity are indeed born in the half-light, half-darkness of the mind. These "seeds of light" live a mysterious, hidden life there—which entails no diminution of spiritual energy. On the contrary!

Jacques Maritain has established the existence, in each human soul, of a spiritual unconscious. He writes: "Our intellect is fertilized by intelligible seeds, on which depends the entire formation of ideas. . . . But it knows nothing of these seeds that it receives, nor even of the process by which it produces its concepts. Thus, this original Source of light remains invisible to us, hidden in the unconscious of the mind."[44] And yet, the idea of being and the principle of identity of being,

which the intellect pronounces before all things, arouse, penetrate, and activate all of our intellective cognition. How
astounding, these beginnings of the life of our mind, which
are nevertheless hidden from our mind!

Were we to trace the source of a river that spreads out, all
majestically, into an ocean that washes the coast of our conti-
nent, first by going upstream from the mouth of the river,
then from the river to a stream, then to a rivulet, then to a sil-
ver little trickle, and thence to the source—how astonished we
would be to find, as the source of our mighty river, springing
from beneath an ice cap, myriad droplets of water, flowing day
and night, far from the view of human beings, in the silence
of the ice caps. So it is with the ocean of truths discovered by
human beings. All have, as their ultimate source, two principles. These two principles never cease giving their light as
being within reason, in our spiritual supra-consciousness.

This region of the mind is situated where all of the faculties
of knowledge emerge, still linked to the soul. They envelop
one another. The first two principles, which spring up from
the soul at its source are caught, swept, into the torrent of sen-
sations and images. But by virtue of their pure spiritual light,
these lightning bolts of mind penetrate the outward senses
and the flood of images from end to end.

It is to these regions of the mind in particular that one must
go "upstream" if we wish to understand the first religious intuitions of the human being. It is in the profound chasms of this
supra-consciousness that, for example, the primitives formed
the myths of creation. From its first emergence, the intellect is
found ordered to being. It is this first, basic act—snatching
things from nothingness—that has been felt as an act of
instinct. By instinct, the intelligence of the primitives felt that
the world and the things that array it maintain a relationship
of dependency with a being who is invisible, but all-powerful
and all-knowing.

From the immense fund of the data of the history of religions, let us cite only this one, confided to Rasmussen by an Eskimo shaman: "I believe in a powerful spirit, preserver of the universe, governor of the weather, so mighty that his word to human beings cannot be understood in ordinary syllables, but must be expressed by rainstorms, snowstorms, tidal waves, and all of the forces human beings fear."[45]

As we see—and this emerges most emphatically in religious myths in particular—it is not necessary that the idea of being become conscious and reflexive in order to be operative. Still, it is obviously because of this idea and its first demands, present in the unconscious of the human mind, that the world of things that are born and that die postulates the existence of a transcendent cause. For many thousands of years, the path of the intuitions of the mind was the only way human beings had to lead them to a God who had created the world. Among the Algonquins of the forests of the Northeast, religious science has found this intuition: "He created things by joining his hands and separating them once more. He used neither sand, nor rock, nor limbs of trees to make human beings. He thought, simply, and they existed."[46] In the background of these recitals, and of so many others like them, is hidden the concept of being, and its formidable might of divine light.

Then, one day, another trail—that of a philosophical intelligence conscious of its sources—was blazed. It too led to God. We know the date of this event, one of the most important in human history. In the sixth century B.C., Parmenides, a Greek philosopher living at Elea, in southern Italy, produced, in clear consciousness, a structured doctrine of being and its properties. And on that day, the metaphysics of being was born.

36

Parmenidean Being: A Bouquet of Stars

The intelligence is kindled the day it wonders what it is to be. It finds its most immediate response in its own deepest heart. It becomes aware that it knows one thing: the intellect knows nothing but being and what has intrinsic rapport to being. And on the simplicity of this point, as upon an invisible ruby, it balances the universe.

—Dom Vermeil

HUMAN INTELLIGENCE DID NOT await Parmenides in order to "think being." But before him—and after him, besides, more often than not—it thought it insofar as it is realized in such or such a sensible thing. For example: "This oak here. . . ." And it is apropos of being in a bodily thing that it pronounces the first principles of things. "This oak is." It is what it is. It cannot at the same time be and not be what it is. This law of the identity of being is held by all intelligence—by that of the aboriginal, the child, the civilized person, the adult. This is the very being of which the metaphysician will speak. Only, with the ordinary person, it is present under a mask, and not "disengaged for itself." Well does Jacques Maritain say that it is upon the being of things that common sense relies to get to God: "Unless one considered being in things, one could not pass to the first Cause of all being."[47]

But that of which we wish to speak now is the historic

127

moment of the discovery of being for itself. From this point of view, Parmenides—at least according to the texts that we have—was the first to pose himself the question, What is being? For this act—for that which all things do, and do first, the act of opposing themselves to nothingness—Parmenides was the first to employ the Greek term *to on* in characterizing a thing. It is the present participle neuter of the verb "to be," and would be translated, therefore "being," that is, a body doing the act of being. Parmenides was the first to ask himself how to designate, in language, a thing in a state of being. But the response he receives suddenly transports his mind to the very sphere of the divine. We find these answers in the fragments of a poem. They spring from his mind like a bouquet of light. At the entryway of the temple of philosophical wisdom, they stand like caryatids! Let us gather a few of his most celebrated aphorisms:

> "Being is and non-being is not"—
> therein lies the pathway of certitude,
> and the truth that accompanies it.
>
> There are a thousand proofs that being
> neither is begotten nor perishes.
> I shall not permit you to say, nor to think,
> that it comes from nonbeing, or that
> being is not. . . .
>
> Being is ever indivisible,
> since it is altogether identical with itself. . . .
> It is ever immobile. . . .
> And it abides without changing in its being,
> in itself and by itself, identical.[48]

Let us attempt to understand why Parmenides speaks thus of being. Let us pose ourselves this problem: What could I say of being, of the act of being, by means of reasoning alone, without looking at things?

Just as the idea of the square cannot be other than that of "a polygon with four equal sides and four equal angles," so also the idea of being implies that the nature of being is being. But then, it cannot not-always-be. Thus, it has not begun, and cannot end. In consequence, it is eternal. It is necessary, as well. Finally, we must say that being is immobile. It cannot acquire being, since then it would have lacked being. But this is impossible for being.

What had happened to the "father of metaphysics" was unheard of! He had been searching for the properties of the being that, as with everyone, was there before his eyes. And he must pronounce attributes of the divine being! Arriving at this peak, where his thought had lifted him, and then returning to the world, he could not find there enough consistency to be able to attribute to things that come into being and then are not, the attribute of "being." The idea of being had flashed so brightly that it had obliterated things! The concept of being, the first concept of all, and its law of identity—these two seeds of light in every intelligence—in the mind of Parmenides had suddenly yielded their divine promise. God, as Gilson observes, had arrived in the being of metaphysics.[49]

37

Beings Bear Witness to Being

You are a fish
from the great depths.
Luminous and blind, . . .
you, you do not deceive.
You avoid no detour.
You rise when you please,
from where you please. . . .
You do not ascend by machine.
You ascend, like a cork,
toward the regions that have need of you.
            —Jean Cocteau to Jacques Maritain

CONSCIOUSLY OR NOT, the intellect is essentially ordered to being. It is for being that it hungers. But its first taste is for the being that is in sensible things. Linked intimately to its body, the intellectual soul first opens its eyes to being clothed in matter: the being of this oak, of this rose.

But in this second part, we shall no longer speak of being as the act by which a thing builds up its body with matter. We shall now speak of the act by which it emerges from nothingness and holds itself above nothingness. We speak, then, of the being that comes from beyond matter, from farther away than matter. Now we are dealing with metaphysical being. *Meta,* in Greek, means "beyond."

Now, metaphysical being is grasped in many ways. Common sense itself grasps it, but after a fashion that is like groping in the dark. Still, it is thanks to this apprehension that a prephilosophical affirmation of God is rendered possible. And this affirmation of the natural knowledge of God is at the basis of the religious phenomenon in humanity.

Then there is the apprehension of the act of being in a pure intellectual consciousness, as with Parmenides. Now being is seen for itself, as if unmasked. We have seen how the intellect finds itself suddenly propelled toward God. But this was at the price of the negation of the sensible world. Tradition has retained statements in which Parmenides refuses to ascribe existence to things: "The senses are deceivers." And: "One must struggle with deceitful illusions."[50] His blazing intuition effaces the world. Parmenides is lifted toward God by a *deus ex machina*—and the machine is that of logic alone.

A century and a half after Parmenides, Aristotle too opened philosophical routes to God. But he began with the world. Being, to his eyes, was apprehended first in sensible things. Against Parmenides, Aristotle said: "One must understand 'being' in manifold senses." For one, individual bodies have the right to be called "beings," "be-ers." This tree, this bird, this rose hold themselves above nothingness in themselves. Aristotle, however, acknowledged that the energy of being, in these things, was subject to death. The being he considered made its apparition by birth and disappeared by death. It is between these two terms, then, that things truly perform the act of being. Now, it is upon these beings that metaphysics will stand in order to reach all the way to God.

For St. Thomas Aquinas, who has so scrutinized existence— things' act of being—the metaphysician is indeed a "fish from the great depths." After all, in the ocean of the things of this world, metaphysicians descend all the way to this fundamental act and remain there. Each beginning of something they experience as a snatching from nothingness—a miracle! But each death, each disappearance—is as a disaster!

> What would they do, my God—
> all of these poor things that subsist
> only by their nature, which is to come into being
> and to cease to be—
> in order to testify that you are at both terms!
> Would that they could die away from our eyes
> without lacerating the heart![51]

But before testifying to the existence of God, things, whose "nature . . . is to come into being and to cease to be," testify to an essential fragility, to a radical impotence before existence. In the constituents of their essence, we do not find existence. Existence in them is really distinct from their essence. Since they are born, they can only receive it. Since they die, they cannot keep it.

And yet, essence in things, as we have seen, bespeaks a fantastic energy. It works so vigorously, to realize, for example, its "rose program," its "oak program," its "titmouse program"! But it cannot "real-ize" its existence. Existence is not in its program as an act to be performed, but only as an act to be received. In the ocean of things in which the metaphysician descends to the bottom of their being, in none of them does that metaphysician find the cause that makes them to exist. Then,

> Like the fish in the running water,
> which swims upstream, swallowing,
> the one attached to you
> struggles against the grain of time.[52]

Ordered to being like sight to color, the intellect seeks a reason for the existence of these things. Of all of these contingent beings, that are born and die, it searches out the cause of existence. It well sees that none of them has had enough strength to emerge from the abyss of nothingness. Beneath them there is nothingness.

It is then that metaphysicians rise out of this world like a cork, since in this world they cannot render any adequate account of its existence. The intellect must therefore rise beyond this world of contingent beings. It rises "like a cork" beyond all these things and goes in search of their Cause. But this cause can only be the being whose essence bears a demand for existence. The Being beyond beings! Nothing, indeed, can come from nothingness to being but by the Being in which nothingness has no place.

38

From the Being-with-Nothingness to the Being-without-Nothingness

I have not yet begun to speak,
and behold, Yahweh,
you know my speech altogether.
    You hem me in behind and before,
you have placed your hand upon me.
                                        —Psalm 138:4–5

WHY IS IT NECESSARY to emerge from this world in order to render account of the existence of the things that are in this world? Why could things not communicate existence to, share existence with, one another? They are the source of so many benefits to one another. The sun lavishes its light and warmth. The bird rejoices the countryside with its song. The rose casts abroad its perfume. Why would they not have the power to make the gift of existence?

In order to respond to these questions, we must first of all observe that no thing of this world can "incorporate" existence. Existence is no more in their power after receiving it than before. Existence is not in the program they have to achieve. True, existence gives the things of this world—this rose, this marigold—to realize the program inscribed in their nature. But precisely, to produce existence is not inscribed there. If existence were to be the "property" of things, we would be sure that they would keep it forever, as it is the most precious gift they have. But the death of things—as we have said—marks their radical impotence to exist of themselves. No, existence is given them, ever and anew.

St. Thomas Aquinas uses an image to render this doctrine more understandable. He compares existence to the light of the sun, and the essences of this world to the air the sunshine penetrates (see *STh* I, q. 104, a. 1). In virtue of its diaphanous character, air is the matter the most suited to receive the light of the sun. But in virtue of the same diaphanous character, it is also the element with the least capacity for retaining it. Let the sun withdraw, and the air is dark in an instant. Anyone who has lived in the tropics knows that it takes but a scant quarter-hour for brightest day to give way to total night.

That is the way it is with the things of our universe when it comes to existence. Their essences do not have within them the power to keep it. Water, for example, retains the heat it has received, and communicates it. Not having existence in their power to keep, the things of our universe stand in constant need of the influx of God, the Sun of being. The air remains illumined only if the sun shines on it and in it. Just so, the essences of this world remain in existence only if the being whose essence is to exist creates in them this first of all gifts.

For that matter, the brightened air is not the producer of light, but its vessel, its vehicle, its reflection. But when an essence exists, it is not the vehicle and vessel of existence, but existence is its vehicle, instead, maintaining it above nothingness.

There is a radical, absolute poverty in the things of this world. In the face of existence, they are even more poor than the air before the light. Tenuous and fluid as it is, at least air exists without light. Instead, a thing is as yet *nothing* before the arrival of existence! It appears only when existence snatches it from the original night of nothingness. Thus, this swarm of beings that people the universe have need of the continual influx and support of the First Cause of existence. At each breath, they must be supported by the omnipotent hand of God, the self-existent. This causal influx plunges to the depths of their being, ceaselessly producing the existence that bears them. St. Thomas Aquinas celebrates existence: "Existence is in each thing, and is more intimate, more profound, more fundamental than anything else that constitutes it" (*STh* I, q. 8, a. 1).

Metaphysics, as we see here, is not in competition with biblical revelation. It is metaphysics that creates the best exegesis of the biblical poems consecrated to the creative action of God. Psalm 139 tells us, in lavish, penetrating images, how very close—precisely because of the constant gift of existence— God always is. Having addressed God this verse of praise: "You hem me in behind and before, you have placed your hand upon me," the Psalmist goes on to sing, as if in ecstasy:

> It is you who have formed my loins,
> who have fashioned me in my mother's belly!
> I give you thanks for so many prodigies,
> marvel that I am, marvel that are your works!
> —Psalm 139:13–14

39

From Participated Being in Things to the Perfect Being

A thousand graces scattering,
He passed through these woods in haste,
And casting his regard on them as he went
With only his face
He left them arrayed in beauty.

—St. John of the Cross

AMONG THE PERFECTIONS of which the beings of this world are the vessels, certain ones are limited to a single category: for example, the horse belongs to the category of substance. Or "large," to the category of quantity; "black" to the category of quality. Other perfections, on the contrary, are attributable to all categories. These are the perfections that are called "transcendentals," which have the power to lead the spirit all the way to God.

Being, oneness, truth, goodness, beauty, are words "built in a pyramid," said Ramuz. Seized first in things here below, these perfections feed the spirit. But they whet even more its hunger for the infinite. They appear to the mind on the face of things, but they make it desire another Face, where these attributes glisten. Since, of themselves, they involve no limitation to a category, they summon the soul to ascend to its true homeland.

> A cry repeated by a thousand sentinels,
> An order resounding through a thousand horns.[53]

Among these perfections, let us take, by way of example, beauty. This is the transcendental in which one best grasps the call addressed to the spiritual soul to leave this world. Baudelaire evokes its power of attraction by comparing it to a lighthouse orienting a vessel toward the port of desire: "It is a beacon, kindled upon a thousand citadels."[54]

Beauty reveals to the poet its secret procedures. Because poets consume their days in its pursuit, it takes them into its confidence:

> To seduce these docile lovers,
> I have some pure mirrors,
> that make all things more beautiful:
> my eyes, my great eyes turned toward eternal lights.[55]

Beauty is found in the "prism" of numberless things, even in opposite things. Lovers of beauty suddenly see it scintillate upon things indifferent to other persons. We have Apolinaire's awe-struck exclamation: "You read advertisements, catalogues, and the notices that sing at the top of their lungs. See therein this morning's poetry!"[56]

This world is a mirror fallen from the skies, shattered into a thousand pieces. In each piece, a bit of heaven is reflected. When, of a sudden, in a fragment, matter shines with a ray emanating from above, human beings are seized with a strange desire. They find it impossible to abide in the multiple, the fragmentary. Lost oneness must be recomposed. Human beings must have this "elsewhere," where the All exists! Here below, in this multiplicity, in the fragmentary, beauty is in exile. Since of itself it implies no limitation, it must have its source in another world.

What we have just said of beauty, we must also say of the other transcendentals. It is all truth, and not just certain ones, that the mind seeks to possess. It is not in some sparse and fugitive goods that the heart wishes to delight, but in happiness. These desires and aspirations offer a touching witness that the human soul feels itself "exiled in the imperfect, and would at once take hold even in this world of a revealed paradise."[57] In *The Brothers Karamazov* Dmitri tells Alyosha, "No, the human spirit is too vast."

Philosophy has reserved a term for defining the status held here below by these perfections that are of themselves unlimited. It calls them, "participated" perfections. They are as it were "left" in a block of marble, on a face, in a melody. Beauty, of itself unlimited, is nevertheless present in its things, but according to a part, merely, a portion. It is received, then, added to many other perfections. It is not here of itself. It is caused here below.

But just because it is nowhere found of itself, here below, the intellect instinctively goes in quest of its Cause. It naturally posits the latter elsewhere, in another Being: where beauty is only beautiful, where truth is full, where goodness is satisfying, where oneness is indivisible—in the being in which all of the transcendentals are joined.

Among the philosophers who have most keenly felt that the participation, the fragmentation of these perfections vehemently demand the possession of the plenitude of what they announce, we must cite Plotinus—a Greek philosopher who lived in the third century A.D. He counsels the lover of beauty nothing less than flight to the homeland:

> Let us take flight for our dear homeland. . . . Our homeland is the place whence we have come, and our father lives there. For this journey, we need prepare neither team nor ship. We need only cease to look about, and, closing our eyes, exchange this manner of seeing for another, and awaken this faculty that all possess, but few use. (*Enneads* I)

That "faculty that all possess, but few use" is the eye of the soul, which silences images, memory, and shadows.

40

The Hidden Spring

*A*ristotle sees God in the world.
                    —Père Festugière, O.P.

"To see God in the world."[58] This phrase is an apposite summary of the direction in which metaphysics leads the intellect when the latter undertakes to examine and analyze being. And it is the glory of Aristotle to have opened the way.

The Greek thinkers of the fifth and sixth centuries B.C. are the ones who initiated this "questioning" on the being of things. What especially fascinated them was being, but being in the time of its origins. Observing the process of formation, certain among them could not escape the thought that a Being-beyond-the-world was at work. Metaphysics opens the eyes of the mind, and shows, in the history of being, certain phenomena of such worth that being could not have bestowed them upon itself.

Aristotle pursued this quest and observed these processes more scientifically. The outcome only confirmed this feeling. In his *On the Parts of Animals,* his "discourse on method," he cannot conceal his admiration for nature's constructions, in particular at the "plan" it had invented. And he enthusiastically endorses his predecessor Anaxagoras's affirmation that a "spirit" (*Nous*) presides over the formation of things. "When someone says that there is in nature, as with animals, an 'intelligence' at work, the cause of order and of the universal arrangement, this person is seen to be the only sane one." Yes, in this organization of matter there appears a governing idea. In this intelligent energy, God is manifest as in a mirror!

The "ingenious" side of being in its formation is not the only character that requires its attachment to another Being, a transcendent being. For Aristotle, the most decisive character may be that the movement of ontogenesis is a becoming that grows richer from step to step. The progressive aspect of this vital evolution arrested him even more. In appearance, one could think that, in the course of this process, the more emerges from the less. Unable to admit a like contradiction, Aristotle ascribed these passages from the lesser to the greater to a hidden source. It is this invisible cause that brings to act what is as yet merely potency. Accordingly, he posited, above these processes, what in his language he called the Prime Mover. The Prime Mover is the principle of all movements from less to greater. Universally responsible for all passages from potency to act in nature, the Prime Mover is beyond the world: the incorporeal, immaterial agent, pure act.

Alongside the progressive character of the processes of genesis of the nature of things, Aristotle was also struck by the dynamism that envelops seeds, for example, and bears them with rapidity toward their ends. One can sum up the impression produced by the organism thus built up by saying: Not only does being emerge from its Cause, rather it goes toward it! Behind such attractions, the philosopher detects, in every being of this world, a natural love for Pure Act, which is also the Supreme Good. This love nourishes this directed dynamism. Because it loves transcendent Being more than itself, since it depends on it, the living organism activates itself, to form, in this world, likenesses of the perfect Being. It is by this same love of God, implanted deep within participated beings, that evolution is explained. It explains the dynamism of a matter that tends to transcend already existing forms and move toward other, more perfect forms—toward ever higher images of the universal Good.

Finally, the greatest of the perfections to be found in the things of this world is also the one that demands most insistently its attachment to the perfect, Necessary Being. This perfection is existence, the act of acts. As the greatest energy of being, it makes things emerge from nothingness! Existence is a veritable miracle. The death of things loved often plays a revelatory role. That is when we grasp their irremediable frailty. The metaphysician calls this frailty their "contingence." Sometimes with a sensation of anguish, sometimes with a sensation of joy at the birth of beings, we realize that existence here below is always threatened. The being of things is borrowed, begged. It has been said: "The contingence of the universe does not have enough consistency in order to resolve, by itself, the problem of its existence. It sends us back to something else. The world drives us out of itself, drives us above itself, in order to find the reason for this universe. It has enough consistence to exist, not enough consistence to explain itself."[59] Indeed, it can only explain itself by a Being that is not of this world, since, here below, being is subject to birth and death. It can explain itself only by the Being to which existence belongs by essence: the self-subsistent Being, the Being we call "God."

Jean Cocteau gave a riveting image of the metaphysician when he wrote to Jacques Maritain: "You ascend, like a cork, toward the regions that summon you." Maritain, for his part, has found an even more suggestive image. He compares the metaphysician to the seabird that, to find its nourishment, plunges into the ocean of sensible things. But what meta-physicians discover at the depths of being is a magic mirror! "It is as if by dint of plunging into the ocean, one ended by finding, at the bottom, a magic mirror reflecting heaven. Then the gaze is reflected on high, toward purely intelligible objects."[60]

Herein resides the grandeur of this calling: to plunge deep enough into things—to their very being—as to see God there—God who has left on things the divine signature, and has made known by this signature the divine origin of the world.

Conclusion

I turn toward the intelligence of the Pater Omnipotens.
—Paul Cézanne

METAPHYSICIAN AND ARTIST meet before the profoundest mystery things conceal. Our book will have shown that. We must conclude, then, that both of them deal with being. But one must add at once that this relationship to being is very different with the one and the other. The metaphysician feels called to contemplate, in things, their act of being and its varied, inexhaustible richness. The artist feels the need to create beings. The artist brings into being a universe of objects parallel to things.

Only the metaphysician knows the true worth of the artist, of the vocation of the artist, of the artist's singular destiny amid human beings. And the metaphysician offers us a definition: The artist is the imitator of nature and God.

Aristotle was the first to compare the artist to nature. Everyone knows his celebrated formula, "Art imitates nature" (*Physics* 2.2; 194a21–22). The context in which this sentence echoes makes it clear that Aristotle did not wish to establish a relationship of identity between the respective products of art and nature. He never declared that works of art ought to be copies, duplicates, slavish imitations of things produced by nature. Instead, he located "imitation" in the generative process of both.

Every work of art begins with a creative intuition. It drops into the artist's soul something like a seed of light. The creative idea falls onto the soil of the soul, rich with all the experience of its life. What a novelist confides will be enlightening here. Bernanos writes:

> The moment I take up my pen, what immediately wells up within me is my childhood—my so ordinary childhood, which resembles all others, and from which I nevertheless draw everything I write, my inexhaustible spring of dreams. The faces and countryside of my childhood, all mixed, confused, shuffled by that kind of unconscious memory that makes me what I am—a novelist and, please God, a poet.[61]

The depths of the soul of artists, then, their "unconscious memory," has the role of the prime matter of their work-in-progress. In this reservoir, the creative idea finds the elements to be integrated. The creative idea itself plays the role of "form," and, as Maritain says, "of entelechy of the poem." Like a seed in the soil, the creative intuition mobilizes, draws to itself what the faculties of the soul can furnish it. Then, as a natural organism, in constructing itself, thrusts toward the light, so the idea, by the work of the psyche, also thrusts toward the light. The light in the latter case is the work that appears to the eyes. Braque liked to say: "In art, the seed is the emotion, the work is the bursting of a blossom."

Having said this of art, the metaphysician has not yet said what is most profound. To Aristotle's celebrated formula, the metaphysician will add: Art imitates God, the *Pater Omnipotens*. On this point, the philosopher receives suggestive reflections from artists, modern ones in particular. Rainer Maria Rilke, for example, in a letter written at the age of twenty-eight, documents his conception of art: "In the world, the thing is determined; in art it ought to be more so. Withdrawn from every accident, disengaged from all half-light, ravished from time and delivered to space, it becomes permanence, it attains eternity." In the same letter, he said of Rodin, whom he had watched at work: "Things subject to duration, he took it as his task to adapt to the world—less threatened, more calm, more eternal—of pure space."[62]

The aspiration of the poet, then, the painter, the sculptor, is to bestow more "existence" on the thing that has moved them to their inmost depths. They are tormented by the desire not to describe it, not to reproduce it, but to snatch it from the grip of time. By shaping the thing otherwise than it exists in reality, in transposing it, they seek to withdraw it from death. For Malraux, art is anti-destiny. He wishes first of all to save things. "The great work of art," he said, "is not absolute truth as the artist sees it. It 'is.' It has arisen. It is not completion, but birth."[63] In order to make it "be" outside time, the artist deforms it, geometrizes it, abstracts it, recomposes it.

In this second phase, artists express their creative idea. Then it is that they imitate God. They are moved by the need to create, themselves as well, "their world"—a world where death will no longer have a purchase, a world in which being will be wrenched from nothingness. Art is not necessarily, as is too often said, the will to rival God, to oppose oneself to God. It is rather "imitation of the creative act." "I turn toward the intelligence of the *Pater Omnipotens,*" said Cézanne.

These reflections seem to us to be sufficient to establish that the poet, the painter, the artist, they too, have an immediate rapport with being. To be sure, once more, this rapport differs from the one the metaphysician maintains with being. Both, however, because of this fundamental relationship, would delve into the "professional secrets" of nature and of God, in order to reveal them. Is this not what explains their astonishing kinship in intuition?

Things! The wonderful things of this world! It is with these that this philosophy book has been concerned throughout. The things of this world lie endlessly open to the understanding of the metaphysician and the contemplation of the poet and the painter. When these disclose being, they direct the intellect toward God. When they awaken the depths of the soul, they invite it to create. But their ultimate fragility and irreversible contingence often cause a deep wound in the heart of those whom they have charmed:

> Had their voice not been so moving,
> had they not spoken so well of other things,
> creatures would not put any questions to us,
> and we would be at peace with the rose.[64]

True wisdom would consist in gathering them just as they are, and in accepting the fact of losing them. Have they not actually accomplished their mission when they have set the zealous soul on its course to God? Eventually we must heed this sage advice:

> All of the things of the earth—
> we should love them in their transiency,
> and carry them on our fingertips,
> and sing of them softly,
> keep them, offer them by turns,
> not to hold them for more than a day,
> take them,
> suddenly to hand them in
> like a travel ticket,
> and consent to lose their face.[65]

Notes

Part 1

1. Paul Claudel, *Tête d'or*, première partie (Paris: La Pléiade, 1967), 183. For an English translation, see *Tête-D'or: A Play in Three Acts*, trans. John Strong Newberry (New Haven: Yale University Press, 1929), 22.
2. Francis Olivier, *Ramuz devant Dieu* (Paris: D.D.B., 1975), 130.
3. Antoine Saint-Exupéry, *Citadelle* (Gallimard-Folio), 62–63. For an English translation, see *Wisdom of the Sands*, trans. Stuart Gilbert (New York: Harcourt, Brace, 1950).
4. Heraclitus of Ephesus, in *Les penseurs grecs avant Socrate*, trans. Jean Voilquin (Paris: Garnier), fragment 41.
5. Cited in A. D. Sertillanges, O.P., *La philosophie de Claude Bernard* (Paris: Aubier, 1943), 92.
6. "Lettre d'un Chartreux," *Nova et vetera* (1959): 79.
7. Irving Stone, *La vie ardente de Michel-Ange* (Paris: Plon, 1983), 92.
8. Paul Cézanne, *Musées nationaux* (Paris, 1974), 8.
9. Feigenbaum, seit wie lange schon ists mir bedeutend,
   wie du die Blüte beinah ganz überschlägst
   und hinein in die zeitig entschlossene Frucht,
   ungerühmt, drängst dein reines Geheimnis.
For a complete English translation, see *Duino Elegies*, trans. C. F. MacIntyre (Berkeley: University of California Press, 1968), 45.
10. Jean Beaufret, *Dialogue avec Heidegger: Philosophie grecque* (Paris: Editions de Minuit, 1973), 118.
11. See Maurice Zermatten, *Les dernières années de R.-M. Rilke* (Fribourg: Le Cassetin, 1975), 177.
12. Pierre Desgraupes, *R.-M. Rilke* (Seghers, 1970), 74.
13. Raïssa Maritain, *Poèmes et essais* (Paris: D.D.B., 1968), 125.
14. Vincent van Gogh, *Lettres à son frère Théo* (Grasset, 1937), 51. For

a complete English translation, see *The Complete Letters of Vincent van Gogh* (Boston: New York Graphic Society, 1978).

15. G. Romeyer Dherbey, *Les choses mêmes: L'age d'homme* (1983), 16.

16. Martin Heidegger, *Introduction à la métaphysique*, (Paris: Gallimard, 1967), 81. For an English translation, see *An Introduction to Metaphysics*, trans. Ralph Manheim (New Haven: Yale University Press, 1959).

17. Cited by Marguerite Nicod, *Du réalisme à la réalité* (Paris: Droz, 1966), 171.

18. Van Gogh, *Lettres à son frère Théo*, 74.

19. Saint-John Perse, *Poésie* (Paris: Gallimard, 1961), 2. For an English translation, see *Two Addresses* (New York: Pantheon Books, 1966).

20. Jacques Maritain, *Les degrés de savoir, Oeuvres complètes* (Fribourg: Editions Universitaires, 1961), 4:277. For an English translation, see *Distinguish to Unite: Or, The Degrees of Knowledge* (New York: Scribner, 1959).

21. *Les penseurs grecs avant Socrate*, trans. Voilquin, 29.

22. *Trois contemporains*, trans. Y. Battistini (Paris: Gallimard), 30.

23. *Les penseurs grecs avant Socrate*, trans. Voilquin, 135.

24. Saint-John Perse, *Oiseaux* (Paris: Gallimard, 1963), 21. For an English translation, see *Birds*, trans. Roger Little (Durham: University of Durham, 1967).

25. Charles Journet, in *Nova et Vetera* (1962): 38–39.

26. Dante, *The Divine Comedy: Inferno,* canto 3, lines 4–6.

27. Paul Claudel, *Je crois en Dieu* (Paris: Gallimard, 1961), 29. For an English translation, see *I Believe in God: A Meditation on the Apostles' Creed* (New York: Holt, Rinehart & Winston, 1963).

28. Paul Claudel, *Figures et paraboles: La légende de Prakriti* (Paris: La Pléiade, 1965), 956.

29. Ibid., 954.

30. Yves Coppens, *Pré-Ambules* (Paris, 1988), 26.

31. Stone, *La vie ardente de Michel-Ange*, 92.

32. Stanislas Fumet, *Le néant contesté* (Paris: Fayard, 1972), 123.

33. Claudel, *Figures et paraboles*, 964.

34. Desgraupes, *R.-M. Rilke* (Seghers, 1970), 74.

35. Fumet, *Le néant contesté*, 123.

36. Ibid.

37. Claudel, *Figures et paraboles*, 963.

38. Ibid., 964.

39. Ibid., 965.

40. Georges Borgeaud, *Le soleil sur Aubiac* (Grasset, 1987), 58.

41. See Zermatten, *Les dernières années de R.-M. Rilke*, 150.

42. Claudel, *Tête d'or*, 182.

43. *Les penseurs grecs avant Socrate*, trans. Voilquin, 77.
44. See Zermatten, *Les dernières années de R.-M. Rilke*, 183.
45. C.-F. Ramuz, *Découverte du monde* (Lausanne: Mermod, 1951), 90–91.
46. Jacques Maritain, *Sept leçons sur l'être*, 5:581. For an English translation, see *A Preface to Metaphysics: Seven Lectures on Being* (New York: Sheed & Ward, 1958).
47. Jacques Maritain, *Courte traité de l'existence et de l'existant*, 9:29. For an English translation, see *Existence and the Existent* (Westport, Conn.: Greenwood Press, 1975).

Part 2

1. Eugène Ionesco, *La quête intermittente* (Paris: Gallimard, 1987), 20.
2. Alexander Solzhenitsyn, *Le premier cercle* (Laffont, 1968), 20. For an English translation, see *The First Circle* (New York: Bantam Books, 1969).
3. Francis Jammes, quoted by Ernest Dutoit, *Domaines: Les idées et les mots* (Fribourg: Editions Universitaires, 1960), 118.
4. Maritain, *Sept leçons sur l'être*, 5:617.
5. Ionesco, *La quête intermittente*, 106.
6. Paul Claudel, *Cinq grands odes: L'esprit et l'eau* (Paris: La Pléiade, 1957), 238. For a complete English translation, see *Five Great Odes*, trans. Edward Lucie-Smith (London: Rapp & Carroll, 1967).
7. Rilke, *Duino Elegies*, the sixth elegy:
   Feigenbaum, seit wie lange schon ists mir bedeutend,
   wie du die Blüte beinah ganz überschlägst
   und hinein in die zeitig entschlossene Frucht,
   ungerühmt, drängst dein reines Geheimnis.
   Wie der Fontäne Rohr treibt dein gebognes Gezweig
   abwärts den Saft und hinan: und er springt aus dem Schlaf,
   fast nicht erwachend, ins Glück seiner süßesten Leistung.
8. Jean-Paul Sartre, *La nausée* (Paris: Gallimard, 1938). For an English translation, see *Nausea*, trans. Lloyd Alexander (New York: New Directions, 1964), 133, 127, 129, 135.
9. Ibid., 133.
10. Ibid., 129.
11. Ibid., 133.
12. Joseph Chiari, *Picasso* (Buchet/Chastel, 1981), 98.

13. Jacques Chessex, *Maupassant et les autres* (Ramsay, 1981), 126–27.

14. Simone Grengg, *Porion: Souffles, reflets* (Paris: D.D.B., 1977), 53.

15. Maritain, *Sept leçons sur l'être*, 5:592.

16. Claudel, *Cinq grands odes: L'esprit et l'eau*, 238.

17. Ibid., 281–82.

18. Pierre Reverdy, *Le gant de crin* (Paris: Flammarion, 1968), 14.

19. Ernest Dutoit, *Domaines: les idées et les mots*, 95.

20. "Fr. M. C. Reverdy ou la poésie à l'extrême pointe du réel," *Nova et vetera* (1990): 65.

21. Charles Baudelaire, *Sur mes contemporains* (Paris: La Pléiade, 1961), 705.

22. Ibid.

23. Ibid.

24. Ramuz, *Découverte du monde*, 201.

25. Charles Baudelaire, *Correspondances* (Paris: La Pléiade), 11.

26. Baudelaire, *Elévation*, 10.

27. Ibid., 11.

28. Marianne Moore, as cited in Jacques Maritain, *Creative Intuition in Art and Poetry* ("Bollingen Series" 35.1; New York: Pantheon Books, 1953), 330.

29. *Douze questions posées à Jean Beaufret*, 59.

30. Martin Heidegger, *Concepts fondamentaux* (Paris: Gallimard, 1985), 85. For a complete English translation, see *The Fundamental Concepts of Metaphysics: World, Finitude, Solitude* (Bloomington: Indiana University Press, 1995).

31. Guillaume Apolinaire, *Alcools* (Seghers), 54. For a complete English translation, see *Alcools*, trans. Anne Hyde Greet (Berkeley: University of California Press, 1965).

32. Quoted in Olivier, *Ramuz devant Dieu*, 71.

33. Claudel, *Cinq grands odes: La maison fermée*, 283.

34. *Cinq grands odes: L'esprit et l'eau*, 238.

35. *Les penseurs grecs avant Socrate*, trans. Voilquin, 78.

36. *Journal de Raïssa*, ed. Jacques Maritain (Paris: Desclée, 1963), 147. For an English translation, see *Raïssa's Journal*, ed. Jacques Maritain (Albany: Magi Books, 1975).

37. Olivier, *Ramuz devant Dieu*, 136.

38. Ibid., 144.

39. Angelus Silesius, *Le voyageur chérubinique*, book 5, no. 60. For a complete English translation, see *The Cherubinic Wanderer*, trans. Maria Shrady (New York: Paulist, 1986).

40. *Journal de Raïssa*, 147.

41. Jules Supervielle, *"Un poète,"* as quoted in Maritain, *Creativê Intuition in Art and Poetry*, 156.

42. Paul Claudel, *L'annonce faite à Marie*, act 4, scene 5. For a complete English translation, see *Two Dramas: Break of Noon (Partage de midi) and The Tidings Brought to Mary (L'annonce faite à Marie)*, trans. Wallace Fowlie (Chicago: H. Regnery Co., 1960).

43. Etienne Gilson, *Les constantes philosophiques de l'être*, (Paris: Vrin, 1983) 85.

44. Jacques Maritain, *Creative Intuition in Art and Poetry*, 90.

45. J. Goetz, S.J., *Les religions des primitifs* ("Je sais. Je crois"; Paris: Fayard), 60.

46. Ibid., 56.

47. Maritain, *Sept leçons sur l'être*, 5:556.

48. *Trois contemporains*, 60.

49. Gilson, *Les constantes philosophiques de l'être*, 178.

50. *Trois contemporains*, 113 and p. 102.

51. Claudel, *La messe là-bas*, 499.

52. Ibid., 501.

53. Baudelaire, *Les phares* (Paris: La Pléiade), 13.

54. Ibid.

55. Ibid., 20.

56. Apolinaire, *Alcools*, 54.

57. Baudelaire, *L'art romantique*.

58. Père Festugière, *La Révélation d'Hermès Trismégiste*, Vol. 2, *Le Dieu cosmique* (Paris: Librairie Lecoffre, 1949), 227.

59. Cardinal Charles Journet, *Entretiens sur le mystère chrétien*, 1:148.

60. Jacques Maritain, *La Philosophie de la Nature*, 5:850.

61. Quoted in Max Milner, *Georges Bernanos* (Paris: Desclée, 1967), 200.

62. See *Poètes d'aujourd'hui* (Seghers), 168.

63. André Malraux, *Les voix du silence* (La Galerie de la Pléiade, 1951), 459. For a complete English translation, see *The Voices of Silence*, trans. Stuart Gilbert (Garden City, N.Y.: Doubleday, 1953).

64. Claudel, *La messe là-bas*, 500.

65. Anne Perrier, in *Nova et vetera* (1955): 45.